A POSITIVE BIRTH

AARON K. & RILEY

ADAM R. & WINNIE

ADAM S. & FAMILY

ADAM W. & MILLIE

ALEX & OLIVIA

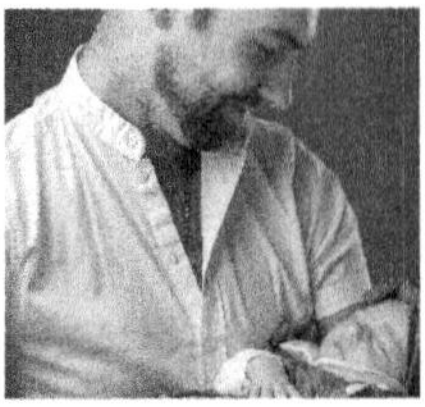

BEN G. & WILLOW

BEN H. & RUNE

BEN L. & JOURNEY

BRION W. & KIDS

JACOB C. & KIDS

JAMES C. & OSWIN

JITENDER S. & IRIS

JOE S. & LUNA

JOHN H. & NORA

LAURIE A. & JUNO

LEWIS J. & BEATRICE

MIKE B. & ARTHUR

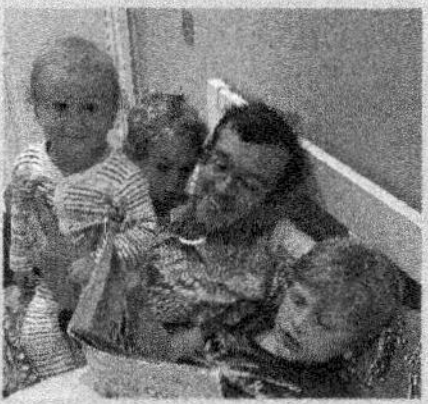

PHIL L. & KIDS

PIERS C. & O.

SIMON F. & OLAF

SIMON H. & TWINS

VIJAY J. & DAUGHTER

WE'VE INTERVIEWED A VARIETY OF DADS AND DADS-TO-BE TO BRING YOU THEIR INSIGHTS AND EXPERIENCES WHEN IT COMES TO HYPNOBIRTHING. SOME OF THEM ARE PROFILED HERE THAT YOU WILL READ ABOUT FIRST HAND ACROSS THE BOOK.

A MASSIVE THANK YOU TO THEM ALL FOR SHARING THEIR STORIES & LEARNINGS.

TWO SPECIAL GIFTS FOR OUR READERS

AS A SPECIAL THANK YOU FOR GETTING THIS BOOK, WE'D LIKE TO GIVE YOU:

110 POSITIVE AFFIRMATIONS AND RELAXATION SCRIPTS

A RANGE OF TEMPLATES FOR YOU AND YOUR PARTNER TO EXPLORE AND USE ACROSS YOUR PREGNANCY JOURNEY TOGETHER

+

DAD RECOMMENDED HYPNOBIRTHING PRACTITIONERS

A DIRECTORY OF AMAZING HYPNOBIRTHING CLASSES THAT COME DAD APPROVED, WHAT THEY OFFER, AND WHAT DADS HAVE GOT TO SAY ABOUT THEM

VISIT WWW.DADDILIFE.COM/ HYPNOBIRTHINGTOOLKIT

TABLE OF CONTENTS

INTRODUCTION

"How can I become a better birth partner?"

That's one of the questions our community asks the most. Over the past five years, across dozens of countries, we at *DaddiLife* have tried our best to answer it. We've interviewed people in your shoes – dads-to-be, first-time dads, fathers of two, three, four, or more, and birth partners of every kind from every possible background.

We've listened to stories from dads who have been there to experience natural births, caesarean births, VBACs, water births, planned and unplanned inductions; births at hospitals, at birthing centers, at home; births in a Hazmat suit, on a plane, over video chat, even on the phone while in the car frantically trying to fight through traffic. When it feels like we've finally heard every possible rendition of birth, a new one is told that – either from laughing too hard or just the pure beauty of it – brings a new perspective.

Across all those interviews, conversations, and friendships that have grown our community, we've found that **every birth, like every baby, is unique**. And no matter how many births we as dads have been a part of, we always want to find a way to do better for our partners on the next one. We want answers to the questions running through our head like:

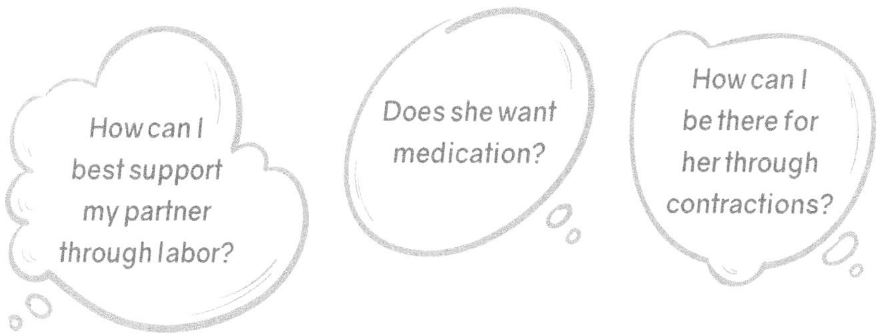

Sometimes dads and their partners aren't as prepared for the challenges of birth as they'd like to be. Sometimes things happen during labor where they or their partners have felt lost, ignored, out of control, steamrolled – even hurt. And as much as we'd like them to be, those funny and uplifting stories aren't the only ones we hear.

Often, we've found that "beautiful, magical, wonderful" are phrases that we as dads hide behind rather than express what birth *actually* felt like to us. Because as many stories as we've been told that renew and refresh us to the possibilities of birth – the first cry that came after a mother's soothing touch, or the son that came out peeing on the doctor, the dad, and everyone in range – we've also heard stories that remind us of the very real challenges of pregnancy, labor, birth, and postpartum.

We've heard about the many birth plans that didn't come to fruition in the delivery room – about the interventions that made dads and their partners feel powerless – about the constant anxieties of not knowing what to do, what to say, or how to help. Worst of all, we've heard stories that framed the entire birth experience for these dads and their partners as something negative – a bad memory or a trauma they try not to dwell on. As something they try to move past, to heal from psychologically as well as physically.

The unfortunate thing that isn't talked about enough is how rare a *positive birth experience* can actually be. It's been estimated that as many as **1 in 3** women will experience birth trauma. Without proper treatment, nearly 10% of those women have symptoms of post-traumatic stress disorder (PTSD) due to that trauma. This isn't always in regards to physical injuries suffered by the baby or the mother either, but rather emotional trauma from the intense experience of birth or interventions during it.

These problems can find themselves cascading too.

Trials from birth can affect mothers afterward, helping contribute to postpartum depression (PPD). As dads, having your partner experience that, alongside a multitude of other anxieties present in parenthood, can have you battling too, feeling mentally and physically on the ropes in the form of paternal postnatal depression (PPND).

And it's made us ask ourselves: *why can't this be better?*

Why is an experience that should be amazing and life-changing be so painful to think about for so many? Why is there an expectation on dads, especially first-time dads, to just be the observer, the watcher waiting on the sidelines – unqualified to be involved? Why should the experience of birth be "something we got through" rather than "something we cherished"? Why isn't birth something we and our partners *always* feel in control of, confident through, and empowered by? Why is there a narrative around birth in society and the media that experiences like this, that leave dads and their partners with PPD and PPND or PTSD, should just "be expected"? That this is all just "the way things are"?

Why can't this be better?

After listening to all of those stories, the good and the bad, we think it can be.

If every birth, like every baby, is unique, then **every birth has the potential to be a positive experience.** It sounds simple, almost like a declaration we're willing into existence – but bear with us and you'll see that birth doesn't have to be "drug-free" or natural; it doesn't have to be a caesarean birth, an induction, or water birth to be a positive experience. No matter where you are and how you choose to give birth, *all* births have the potential to be positive for you and your partner. The difference is how you prepare yourselves and what you do, as a team, to help make it that way.

And that's what we're here to help with.

WHO ARE DADDILIFE BOOKS

DaddiLife Books is the publishing division of DaddiLife – the leading platform and community for modern-day dads. Formed five years ago with a mission to shine a light on the generational change of modern-day dads, the team has written about a number of topics, issues, and opportunities in the area and has grown to a community of over 150,000 dads.

Check us out at www.daddilife.com

A PATH TO POSITIVE BIRTH

Whether you're a first-time dad or a dad of five, we can't really guess what brought you here. There are far too many wonderful, unexpected, and patiently planned paths to fatherhood. But we can tell you *why you're here*. You're here, reading this book and starting these proactive steps, because *birth* and the *experience of birth* will both last a lifetime – but they are two fundamentally different concepts.

As the old adage says, they're two sides of the same coin.

We like to think of *birth* as the physical wellbeing of your partner and the baby as they both perform the physiological efforts to a) birth a human, and b) to be born. This is what doctors and midwives have at the very top of their list of priorities. *Are the baby and the mother physically healthy? Are they physically safe and performing this incredible act in an acceptable range of predetermined parameters?*

The *experience of birth*, on the other hand, is what happens to your partner before they go into active labor. It underpins the birth as it's their prior feelings on pregnancy and about being a parent; it's what happens to them during labor, the interventions given; it's all of their thoughts, actions, and emotions; it's what kind of care and support you offer before and during the birth; it's how you felt through all of it, and it's how you both feel post-birth as well as years down the road.

Obviously, you want your partner and baby to be physically safe and healthy. That goes without saying. However, physical health in this context of birth is short-term. The doctors and midwives have to think in the short-term. They have to make decisions that will offer the best immediate outcome for both the mother and the baby.

Sometimes, those decisions can come in the form of *interventions* – actions taken by doctors or midwives to intervene in the birthing process and assist in the delivery. That might mean an unplanned induction or caesarean birth. That might mean that your birth plan, in a manner of speaking (or literally), goes out the window. There is definitely a time and place for interventions and we'll get into that, but even so, you don't have the luxury of only thinking in the short-term. This isn't their lives – it's yours.

It's your family, and you're in this together, for the long-term.

A positive birth is understanding that both sides of that coin are important because only when taken together do they have value. It's one where you take into account the short-term and the long-term. It's a birth where you and your partner **can choose** how you want the process to unfold and feel in control of those choices.

For that to happen, however, decisions have to be made. Sometimes it can be surprising (even overwhelming) just *how many* decisions you have to make, because all of them have the potential to affect how positive the birth experience turns out to be:

Even if you aren't sure what all those mean yet, all of these decisions can show up in any birth, and all can have a lasting impact on both you and your partner in ways you may not be able to predict. That's why it's important to keep them in mind and be aware of them – to make sure they are *decisions*, rather than *things that happen* to you.

But encouraging and supporting a positive birth experience isn't as easy as changing your perspective, or accepting things you don't agree with because you feel like you're supposed to. All of this takes practice and preparation.

And that's where hypnobirthing comes in.

WHAT YOU'RE GOING TO LEARN IN THIS BOOK

This book is broken down into two parts, each containing three chapters.

The **first half** will outline the core tenants (and a little background history) of hypnobirthing, positive birth, the science behind both, and your role as a birth partner through it all. The **second half** will cover the time you're likely finding yourself in right now – the months leading up to birth. In those chapters, you'll see *hypnobirthing* in action as we guide you through the tail-end of the third trimester, and how to put the tools you've learned into practice to ensure they're ready to go for when your partner goes into labor. Not only that, we'll show you how these tools can be carried with you after your baby has been born and how the principles and techniques of hypnobirthing can come in handy in everyday life as a parent.

We divided it into these two parts in order to build a strong foundation, and then see how that foundation can best be applied – but you still might find yourself parsing through to the sections that directly apply to you, and that's okay. We encourage it. We encourage you to use this book in the way that will benefit you the most.

Throughout the book, we'll offer reflections from real dads in our community, advice from hypnobirthing experts, exercises that you and your partner can try yourselves, and a number of other learnings we know will help you in the journey ahead. Whether you're currently undertaking a course or plan to soon (and we have our own dad-approved hypnobirthing directory if you're still choosing), our goal is to help you and your partner feel more confident and in control of the birth experience to give you the best possible chance of experiencing a positive birth. To do that, we're going to provide you with the hypnobirthing tools, techniques, and insights to be the birth partner you want to be, and set up the foundations for fatherhood to start your journey on a positive first step.

And that's where this all begins, the first step. So let's get started!

WHAT IS HYPNOBIRTHING & HOW CAN IT HELP YOU?

We like to think of hypnobirthing as the *physiology & psychology of birth*. Or simply, the body and mind of birth. It's the mental practices and practical applications used to help **make the birth experience better**.

One of the most common words that we hear associated with childbirth is "pain." From ancient texts to modern media, the sentiment is clear: *childbirth = painful*. Now, we're definitely not trying to send you down a path of saying, "honey, this book told me childbirth actually *isn't* painful. You're overreacting!" Please, don't do that.

We doubt it will end well for anyone involved, especially you.

What we are trying to do instead is analyze what pain actually is to the body – a neurological response. It's our brain telling us that: "Ow, that stove is hot! Don't touch it." The purpose of pain is to stop us from hurting ourselves, and most of the time it's right on the money. **Pain lets us know that something isn't right with our body.**

The problem, however, is thinking about that kind of pain in the same context as childbirth or labor. "Ow, that stove is hot" pain would have the body send a message to the brain to *stop* labor. When your partner is actually in labor, that's probably the last thing she'll want. She might want labor to end, sure – but she definitely won't want to prolong it, and that's what pain does. The body *wants* labor to progress.

For the safety of your partner and the baby, the baby needs to come out.

During labor, the primary chemical fueling the entire process and encouraging the baby to be born is *oxytocin*. Sometimes referred to as the "love hormone" or the "feel-good hormone," oxytocin is typically released when we're having a good time.

So why on earth does it show up during labor?

In the many studies of "pain-free" birth, labor, from a neurological perspective, is the mother's initial bond with the baby being developed. It's the hormones preparing their brain for a unique and loving connection in future interactions. It's the idea that if oxytocin is allowed to help progress labor naturally, without interruption, then the feelings women get during labor may be intense and powerful – but they won't necessarily just be "painful." We aren't here to argue the semantics of "pain-free" birth, but we bring it up because oxytocin is essential during labor to encourage its progression.

The trick is that a lot of different things can impact that progression.

Oxytocin is the feel-good hormone, so when your partner doesn't "feel good," in a manner of speaking, that production can grind to a halt. If your partner feels anxiety, fear, or a loss of control when in the birthing room, then instead of oxytocin, she'll start to produce adrenaline – our "fight or flight" hormone.

Working in tandem with oxytocin and the rest of the complex combination of hormones that encourage labor, your partner's uterus (the womb) is a muscle that is actively trying to push the baby out. In order to function, all of our muscles need blood and oxygen. During labor, when your partner feels calm and is producing oxytocin, the body is functioning as it should be. She may feel those intense, powerful sensations coursing through her body in waves called *contractions* or *surges* that help push the baby out – but again, that shouldn't necessarily be "pain ."Contractions that become progressively more consistent and increasingly intense are a good sign that her uterus is getting the steady supply of blood and oxygen that it needs.

However, if something causes her adrenaline to start producing, that blood and oxygen that was being sent to the uterus to encourage labor will now be sent to her extremities – her arms and legs – so that, from an evolutionary standpoint at least, she can "fight" to protect herself or "flee" to escape the danger.

What this all means is that there are two primary things to be conscious of during labor – **encouraging** the production of oxytocin, and **discouraging** the production of adrenaline. This, as you might imagine, is where you and hypnobirthing come in.

Hypnobirthing is your path to a positive birth and your guide to becoming a better birth partner. By you both learning and incorporating the science of hypnobirthing – taken from a vast area of study, and by implementing various visualizations, affirmations, relaxations, and deep-breathing exercises, you and your partner can work as a team to help focus the mother's mind, and in turn their body, on birth.

The essential role you as a birth partner take on in the hypnobirthing process encourages your partner to stay calm and relaxed - the ideal mode for a safe and positive birthing environment. That mental focus you help your partner cultivate helps oxytocin levels to remain steady and adrenaline levels to stay pretty much non-existent. This, in turn, allows the uterus and other muscles responsible for labor, to focus solely on labor.

"My wife's first labor and delivery was traumatic. Our society just doesn't properly prepare women for childbirth but still lays heavy expectations on them. She used Hypnobirthing for our second two children and it changed everything. I am not exaggerating when I say it changed our lives. I listened to the tracks as well and have even used their other tracks for anxiety, stress, and depression.

- Jacob C. California, US.

"It doesn't help itself in a way because the name suggests hypnotherapy, but at the same time, I would argue that it's more about the education than the therapy part. Because for women who are doing the breathing techniques etc, that's there, but for us dads-to-be, it's more about being the best partner we can, I guess. I didn't really think too much about that. I just was happy to help out in any way I could."

- Joe S. Tonbridge, UK.

> "I found Hypnobirthing great as it arms you with as much knowledge and information as possible. It just meant that on the day, if you heard something said by a doctor or a midwife, you just had a bit more of an idea about what they were talking about. Without that information I think I'd have felt like a rabbit in the headlights!"
>
> - Adam R. Brighton, UK.

WHY "HYPNOBIRTHING?"

"That's all well and good," you say, skeptically. "But why is it called *hypno*birthing?"

As you might imagine, that's another question we get asked often. To clear up any misconceptions as early as possible, hypnobirthing has absolutely nothing to do with *hypnosis*. Nobody is going to pop out of this book, swing a pocket watch in front of your face and say, "you're getting very sleepy and you love hypnobirthing."

First off, who has pocket watches anymore? And second, just imagine the cost! No, honestly, we promise that none of this has anything to do with hypnosis, and most hypnobirthing experts agree that the name could benefit from a bit of a rebrand.

Hey, no better time than the present – our pitch is Medebirthing (from the Greek root 'Mede' meaning *care for* rather than 'Hypno' meaning *sleep*). Or Metabirthing – if Zuckerberg and Facebook can do it, why can't we?

We're just kidding (mostly), but as it stands, the various implications of the name alone (like hippies or hypnotists) have turned more people away from this amazing study and practice than almost anything else. But a name is just a name, and the name put to practice can honestly be life-changing.

And speaking of *practice*, that's where you come in to all of this.

"Initially when I heard the Hypno bit, I was a bit 'I don't know how I feel about that.' But once she explained a bit more about it. I was totally on board with it. When she talked to me about it, and what it actually involved, it made more sense. The title is misleading though. I wouldn't call it hypnobirthing, I would have called it something more like Mindful Birthing. If it had been called that, I'd have been a bit more 'Yeah, I get it.' When I discovered it was more focussed on mindfulness-based exercises and relaxation processes, I was totally on board, especially as we both have that deep interest in psychology, mindfulness, and relaxation."

- Mike B. Pwllheli, Wales

> **"Modern culture has a fairly limited view on birthing - like it can only go a certain way. When it comes to dads, it's just a 'watch and support' role - that's it. But that's so limiting to what it actually can be, and I found that with Hypnobirthing it could be so much more."**
> - Ben H. Hampshire, UK.

GETTING YOU READY FOR THE BIG EVENT

If labor is the big event, gameday, the championship bout, the moment we've all been waiting for, then there's really only one way to prepare for it: **practice**. Your partner already knows a good bit of what to practice – after all, her body has been preparing for this day for nine months. But in order to have the tools to help her, and the knowledge of when those tools are necessary, it's important that you go through the hypnobirthing process alongside her.

Hypnobirthing works best when the pair of you work as a team. If your partner is focused on labor, you're focused on making sure nothing distracts her from that. The reason you're the one most equipped for the job is because it's very likely you're the one who she trusts more than anyone. **You're her biggest source of comfort and reassurance.**

If anyone can make her feel calm, confident, and safe to encourage that production of oxytocin and dissuade that production of adrenaline – if anyone can be the advocate of what she wants most during labor, to ensure it's a positive experience where the many decisions made were her own and consented by her – it's you.

But, as we mentioned, encouraging a positive birth environment and creating the powerful connection that hypnobirthing teaches between the mind, the body, and one another requires some real training. Just like any great gym routine or pump-up Rocky montage, you can't expect to become the better birth partner you want to be without **practice, practice, practice**.

Throughout this book, we're going to help you do just that.

"I never knew that I would be this into the birth. I mean most men don't. It's not a topic of interest. But I was shocked at how interested I was in it all and how beautiful the whole experience was. You know, they call it the miracle of childbirth. And it's like, it's not really a miracle because it's extremely normal and natural. And been going on for a very long time. A lot of people call it a spiritual experience because it's so mysterious and beautiful. And I really was thankful that we really pushed for unmedicated birth because I feel that you get to experience the full bandwidth of, of what birth is all about."

- Ben L. Arkansas, US.

"I do remember thinking, like, oh, God, I'm just going to be useless during pregnancy and birth. You're already anxious about this thing. And then you start thinking, Well, if this is what everyone's saying, then, you know, maybe this is just going to be a disaster. And so I think Hypnobirthing was really, really good for just making sure that I knew that I was important in this and, you know, I've got plenty of responsibilities that I can really help."

- Jitender S. Brighton, UK.

"Sam (my partner) was aware of it, but honestly, I was a bit unsure. It sounded a bit out-there and wacky. I thought to myself, 'does it even involve dads!?' As a dad I wanted to know the science behind birth, but the term Hypnobirthing didn't reflect that at all. But ultimately, I was keen to try it, even if to support Sam. I went into it thinking it wouldn't be for me but ultimately got a lot from it."

- Lewis J. Somerset, UK.

CHAPTER ONE

HYPNOBIRTHING & THE EVOLUTION OF FATHERHOOD

WHAT YOU'RE GOING TO LEARN:

- An understanding of the modern-day dad and the "Father Effect"
- Your role as Guardian of the Cave
- The origins of hypnobirthing
- The origins of our traditions on birth
- An understanding of the "body & mind" of birth

When you think of the word 'dad,' what pops into your head?

For most of us, our mind immediately jumps to our own dads or the father figures in our lives. Our answers, rather than being anything we've ever really had to define, often come from flash-bulb memories, strong feelings, and impactful experiences. Whether good or bad, that's how most of us come to shape our views on fatherhood. We either say, "this is the kind of dad I want to be," or "this is the kind of dad I won't be."

We bring this up because every dad in human history has done this. Generationally, in cultures across the world, children have either seen their father figures and wanted to carry on their traditions, or they've wanted to have those traditions end with them. In many ways, we think of fatherhood as pushing in one direction – forward. But like all of humanity, sometimes it's a tug-of-war.

Right now, most modern dads want to be more involved.

We want to be equal partners and equal parents. We want to change many of the negative traditions that have become engrained in our society: the idea that men are only providers, that we aren't nurturing or caring, that we are inclined to aggression, that we are uninterested in childbirth, or that we have to be biological heterosexual men to be fathers or father*ly* in the first place.

Often, it can feel like those negative perceptions are far behind us. Recent DaddiLife studies show that 87% of modern-day dads are actively involved in the day-to-day care of their children. 68% also have a partner who is working full time – reflecting the rise of dual-income households, and the equalization of parenting occurring all at the same time. However, statistics and culture don't always fall in line with one another, and the transformation of any long-standing tradition is still a tug-of-war.

THE FATHER EFFECT

For a long time, most of the research surrounding paternal care was directly linked to mothers, because they were seen as the primary caregivers of children. That research was important – it gave us new insights into the functions of hormones that we talked about before, the psychological impact of motherhood, as well as the impact mothers can have on their babies. When science did finally turn the spotlight on dads, it was much more concerned with the negative effects of absent and abusive fathers than the positive effects of dads who were present, committed, and involved.

Because of that, the science of fatherhood for a long time fed into the cultural bias, creating a sort of self-fulfilling prophecy for a dad's role in parenting. What's exciting about more recent studies, however, is an increased interest in the positive influence of dads. The main idea of these studies has resulted in something called the "Father Effect" – and it shows the very real impact dads can have on their children at every stage of their lives: from pre-birth through the teenage years and beyond.

Just as the studies about mothers have shown, these studies have discovered a number of hormonal, hereditary, psychological, and physiological aspects of fathers that directly affect their children. It's illuminated how our own oxytocin produces when we bond and directly care for our babies. It's shown how our increased attention and engagement with our children massively increases their cognitive abilities and how our continued support is a fundamental factor in positive development.

More than anything, it outlined one clear conclusion. Involved, loving, and engaged fathers are fundamentally important for the health, wellbeing, and development of their children. What it doesn't tell us, however, is how best to prepare for that role, or that our role begins well before the actual birth of our babies.

This, again, is where hypnobirthing comes in.

The term and concept of hypnobirthing was first coined by U.S. hypnotherapist Marie Mongan in 1989, but the practices of hypnobirthing have been tried and tested not only over the last couple of decades, but over thousands of years of human evolution. It's a culmination of modern insights we never could have had before, and ancient instincts we've all but forgotten. In a sense, what we've found from hypnobirthing wasn't so much discovered, as it was rediscovered through a modern lens.

Nowhere is that clearer than when looking at the roles of fathers from our earliest examples of them – the *Homo Sapiens age* of over 70,000 years ago.

THE MODERN-DAY DAD & THE GUARDIAN OF THE CAVE

Before the Agricultural Revolution 12,000 years ago, early humans lived out their days as hunter-gatherers. The wilds were dangerous, and we didn't yet have all the tools we have today to change that. Although modern evidence suggests we didn't all live in caves, but rather small huts or hovels made of mud and timber or animal bones (yeah, we were hardcore), "cavemen" still has a really nice ring to it.

During that era, as the mother gave birth in the cave (or somewhere private), the partner's role (your role) was to keep them safe. You became the *Guardian of the Cave*, standing stoic and strong by the door, defending her from predators or other threats. The Guardian was tasked with keeping the mother safe during labor and birth, a time in which they would be extremely vulnerable and otherwise unable to defend themselves.

Not to send you off on a daring daydream of fighting saber-toothed tigers or warring Neanderthal factions (even though it sounds pretty exciting), your role hasn't changed as much as it may seem. No, you absolutely do not need to bring your favorite spear to the hospital, birthing center, and definitely not your living room – but you are still there, in any room you find yourself, to keep an eye out for threats.

It's just that, over the years since we lived in caves, the threats have changed.

FOREVER THE GUARDIAN & THE ADVOCATE

When women gave birth in caves, the sound of some looming danger outside might ramp up her adrenaline production and cause her body to slow down or even stop the labor process. As we mentioned, oxytocin is only released when mothers feel safe. When the body realizes that "it's no longer safe, this place is no longer good, we might need to move somewhere else," the brain cranks out adrenaline to cause a "fight or flight" reaction instead.

Back then, defeating the predator or changing locations to somewhere safer (a roomier cave, for example) might have been the only plausible solution. Nowadays, that's far less likely. Where you decide to give birth is likely where you'll stay – but distractions, interruptions, and changes to the atmosphere or the emotions of the mother can still drastically slow down or even pause the labor process. Because of that, you will need to be not only the Guardian of the Cave, but the caretaker of her hormones – and, underlying all of those things, **her advocate,** should the need arise.

That may involve a lot less defending from attacks and far more preventing of interruptions. But every mundane interruption, much like the threat of saber-tooths, gives the same reaction to a mother – "Body, stop the birth right now." To become the most effective birth partner you can be, you have to understand what your partner wants from her birth experience. Luckily, you'll have plenty of conversations before the birth to decide on that, and we'd also encourage you to put together a written and printed birth plan that can be shared with your doctor or midwife so they're all on the same page.

However, sometimes you still won't be on the same page. As much as we'd like it not to happen, it's all too common to sometimes feel at odds with caregivers. Whether from restrictions in a hospital that can't be bent, or standard practices at a birthing center that you and your partner didn't want – conflict can happen in the birthing room. In those situations, where you feel as though your partner's wishes aren't being respected, it's up to you to step up to the plate and advocate for them. That doesn't necessarily mean you need to be directly confrontational, but you do need to make sure your partner's wishes are being heard and advocated for. We'll get into the specifics of these situations later, but just know that this is effectively the modern-day equivalent of fighting off predators, and you're the right guardian for the job.

A MODERN LENS FOR ANCIENT IDEAS

Things have changed quite a bit in 60,000 years, but not as much as it seems. No, you (probably) won't be fighting off a pack of wolves, but you will still need to shield your partner from interruptions. You will still need to make the "cave," whether that's your home, a birth center, or the hospital, feel safe and secure. You will need to encourage her to relax and stay calm, to remind her of how powerful she is in this process and that no one can diminish that power. You will need to support her, believe in her when she finds it hard to believe in herself, be present to her needs, and attentive to her hopes for the birth. You will need to advocate for her while she's in this vulnerable place where absolute focus is required and speak up if her wishes for the birth aren't being respected.

As you go through the practices of hypnobirthing, how exactly you do all of that will become clearer for you. You'll know when to help her into new positions, walk with her to the bathroom, monitor nurses' interruptions, keep family and friends up to date, bring water or food, help keep her calm and relaxed and focused, and much more. Your threats may not be as clear-cut as a predator with extra sharp teeth, but that doesn't mean there aren't any threats to face.

All these years later, you're still the Guardian of the Cave, and you're forever the advocate of your partner's hopes, goals, and desires for a positive birth.

But to do all of that effectively, you have to know what to expect. No matter where you choose to give birth and who you both decide to have in the room with you, you need to be aware of the events and actions that can lead to you and your partner feeling lost, out of control, or steamrolled - all things that make birth trauma or negative feelings about birth more likely to occur.

Just like instincts have cemented themselves in our mind and body from the threats our ancestors faced, traditions can cement themselves too. When it comes to almost any scientific study, tradition and common knowledge are one of the hardest things to overcome. The easiest examples of this to point to are the most obvious. For thousands of years we *knew* for a fact the Sun revolved around the Earth and we *knew* the Earth was flat. Both seem ridiculous now, except maybe to a few YouTubers with way too much time on their hands. But even if the science was sound and proved those long-held beliefs wrong, it still had to overcome tradition and long-held practices.

When looking at the history and science of birth, we face a lot of the same issues. Through evidence-based studies and hypnobirthing, we're discovering new things about birth every day. We're better at understanding the effects of multiple hormones on mothers and babies, the unique bond and changes to physiology in fathers, we're uncovering new practices to encourage positive birth and reduce negative effects postpartum, and we've shown how involved fathers can make an impact at every stage of the process.

But even now, in a more technologically advanced world and scientifically-backed medical community, we can still find ourselves at odds with tradition. Many new studies have shown that immediate cord clamping is dangerous, that forceps and vacuum extractions are medieval, that women should be allowed to eat and drink during low-risk labor, or that the "Golden Hour" is immensely beneficial, when possible, to encourage mother-baby bonding on a neurological and physiological level - yet we can still find ourselves at odds with those long-standing practices.

QUESTIONING TRADITIONS & ENCOURAGING CURIOSITY

At the turn of the 20th century, the divide between births performed by either doctors or midwives was roughly half. However, in the early 1900s "anesthesia" was introduced for pregnancy in hospitals. That decision helped doctors not only pull away from midwives, but from house calls too, as many women came to hospitals sold on the idea of a "pain-free birth." Nowadays, doctors and hospitals perform 90% of all births.

The interesting thing, however, is that for the first half of the century, childbirth wasn't actually "pain-free" and resulted in numerous complications and infections. What was popularized during those years wasn't the epidural or the pain management drugs we know today, but rather the stepping stones to that – unfortunately the stepping stones were just enough drugs (of the questionable kind, like chloroform) to make women completely unconscious during childbirth. As a result, one birth practice first popularized in Germany called "Twilight Sleep" found its way to the U.S. and beyond.

"Twilight Sleep" was a process by which expectant mothers were given enough drugs to fall unconscious for the night, and the doctor forcibly extracted the baby with forceps, allowing the woman to wake up as a new mother. The two drugs used were morphine which caused pain relief and scopolamine (a compound derived from nightshade plants) which caused amnesia. The two combined properly caused women to fall asleep through the "twilight" labor and wake up with no memory of the birth – making it "pain-free."

Unfortunately, "Twilight Sleep" had a number of devastating effects on women. The drugs were often known to cause psychosis with several stories detailing expectant mothers thrashing on their beds, clawing themselves, attacking nurses, or banging their heads on nearby walls – all often happening enough to warrant using strait-jackets and specially designed birthing cots called "labor cribs."

However, as was intended, they often wouldn't remember any of it.

More than that, the negative effect of the drugs also crossed the placenta, impacting the baby's central nervous system. They were often born drugged as a result and unable to breathe without assistance – this is actually where the image of babies held upside down and slapped on the buttocks comes from – it was an attempt to revive them from comas.

Surprisingly, as awful and brutal as this practice was, it went on for around half of the 20th century. It wasn't until early in the Women's Rights movements (the late 1950s – 1960s) that multiple women started to speak out about what they could remember from these birth practices and how barbaric they actually were.

MODERN TRADITIONS & EVIDENCE-BASED BIRTH

We know scientific discoveries in the last century and before have led to remarkable innovations in medicine and breakthrough technologies to make childbirth safer – but, as practices such as "Twilight Sleep" show us, those breakthroughs weren't without their faults. The trouble we face now is that an overreliance on these new technologies has conditioned us to *one* way of thinking about birth – a way that has been colored and reinforced by any number of sitcoms, movies, and secondhand stories over the years. You've heard it before, but let's set the stage:

Labor begins with the water breaking at an inopportune moment, let's say an office Christmas party. Your partner looks at you, and says "the baby is coming!"

You rush off to the hospital, completing your one job as a dad. Once at the hospital, it's a flurried rush to the delivery room after check-in. An orderly pushes your partner away in a wheelchair through swinging double doors as you finish signing all the necessary paperwork.

A few minutes later, you meet them in the delivery room where your partner is already gowned, hooked up to IVs and heart monitors, and labor begins.

Labor goes on for hours and hours.

You and your partner see other new parents come and go, wondering why your baby is taking so long as nurses and doctors constantly check numbers and beeps and adjust IVs.

Finally, after hours of labor, the big moment arrives. Your partner is lying on her back in the hospital bed, already sweating and ready to push as a smattering of individuals come in – more doctors and nurses and onlookers ready to coach her pushing as she screams in pain and "push, push, push!" until the baby comes out. Meanwhile you've been standing somewhere in the corner, probably yelling push too at random times or saying ill-timed jokes until finally the baby is out, the cord is immediately cut, the vernix is cleaned off for photos, the measurements are done, and finally, after the baby is fully documented in the system, it is given back to your partner.

You stand behind her as she holds your baby for the first time and you all huddle close together. That's the whole ordeal, and after it – you're parents.

That story we've been told time and again doesn't completely miss the mark – there is some truth to it. But the best way to describe it is a caricature. It shows a lot of the exaggerated features of labor and birth, but none of the subtle realities.

According to this caricatured story, once you drop your partner off at the hospital, what happens next is out of both of your hands. Her body is the baton in a relay, and the doctors will carry it to the finish line. It can sound impersonal to phrase it like that, but the reason we do is that if you go into birth without any information on how the process unfolds, that's exactly how you might feel by the end.

Things will start to happen and dire decisions could be made due to complications or fear of complications. Everything will start to make you feel like you have no control in the birthing room – that you have no voice that can be heard. This feeling that you're both underqualified to birth a human life, even though for nine months your partner has grown a human life. The assumption is that your baby won't know how to be born, even though it's done a pretty great job of growing without anybody telling it how to.

The real problem with this view is that it paints birth and the experience of birth as black and white. Within it, there's just no grey area. There's no bending on the birth location, the people involved in the room, the instruments or medications used, or the various birthing positions of the mother. There's no prior knowledge on the part of the new parents of possible interventions and what their options are in the face of them. There's a reliance on tradition, conditioned assumptions, and the idea that women know less about what their bodies are feeling at any given moment than the doctors or nurses presiding over them.

The result of this is a series of events that happen to you, rather than a series of steps that you, as a team, take together. And don't forget that the team, in addition to you and your partner, also includes the doctors, doulas, nurses, midwives, and whoever else you want to be involved. You're not supposed to be in conflict with one another, you're supposed to be working toward the same goal – your healthy, beautiful baby, your empowered, healthy partner, and a positive birth experience – together.

As you might've guessed, the goal of hypnobirthing is to remove this *one* way of thinking about birth, and open the door to something "new," evidence-based, science-backed, and better overall for you, your partner, and your baby.

"I think initially, and it's probably the same with a lot of people. It's the name that is a little bit misleading. Initially, I was a bit skeptical, but I didn't realise at the time that it was quite as grounded in science as it is. Initially I thought it would maybe be a little bit wishy washy, because it just sort of didn't sound like it was scientific enough for me. But it was more we were willing to go in with an open mind if that makes sense."

- Adam R. Brighton, UK.

"I guess a lot of people kind of think it like, you know, a hippie-esque thing. I don't know whether I felt that or not. I was quite keen to try it. I had no kind of preconceptions of anything really. But I was interested to try it. With birth itself you have visions of it being painful or being intense. As a dad, and as a guy in the delivery suite you don't want to just be there being pretty useless, and not being able to help in any way just standing there looking like a lost part. I really didn't want that to happen for us."

- Ben G. Worcestershire, UK.

"I think it came from our first pregnancy, where even though it went well and everything like that, my partner thought it was a little bit clinical and she wanted to experience Hypnobirthing going into the next one. So I think from that point of view, she was thinking about what we could do to make it more of a relaxing kind of experience and less clinical. It wasn't so clinical like it was a hospital, it was in a birthing centre with just the midwife the first time, and that's what she wanted again, but she wanted to look at other ways of managing when she was in labor as well. So that's where it stemmed from."

- Mike B. Pwllheli, Wales

"I was in my mid 30s when I found out I was going to become a father. I didn't know what the journey was going to be like. I didn't really think too much more beyond just being as supportive and as good as I could for Charlotte. But then you get to a moment in time when you think; 'well, let's get prepared for what's about to come'. I'm so glad we found Hypnobirthing as it probably brought us even closer together, which we didn't think was possible."

- Piers C. Bristol, UK.

THE BODY & MIND OF BIRTH

Hypnobirthing is an immensely vast study, and with it, there are no one-size-fits-all solutions. We mentioned before that we like to think of hypnobirthing as the *physiology & psychology* of birth. Well, everyone's body is slightly different, as is everyone's mind, and they all work and react differently. A set of techniques that help towards a more positive birth for one woman may not work for another – and that's okay.

The practice isn't limited to one type of person or a particular lifestyle – like we said, it's there for *anyone*. In that way, the value of hypnobirthing comes from how vast a study it is. As you can already start to see, the research into hypnobirthing spans all of human history, and the science of it takes into account every part of human biology.

However, in talking about hypnobirthing, we're conscious that the information we're offering is still directed at you – the birth partner, the first-time dad, or the dad of two, ten, or more. Across this chapter, we've tried to outline a few things:

- That you, as a dad, will have an effect on your child, and it's *your* choices that determine what that effect is
- That your partner has evolved for birth
- That your role in birth starts as the Guardian of the Cave
- That it's vital to understand the possible effects of the important decisions throughout labor and birth before you and your partner make them

- And the last is that **how you talk about birth, matters.**

There's a book out there by Rebecca Dekker, the founder and CEO of Evidence-Based Birth, called Babies *Are Not Pizzas: They're Born, Not Delivered*. It's a fantastic and insightful read overall, and the idea outlined simply in its title is that we *deliver* pizza, newspapers, and mail – but we *birth* babies. It may seem small, but it summarizes something essential to keep in mind moving forward.

As a dad and a birth partner, what we say and how we talk about birth matters to the experience. If we get to a hospital room and hear a nurse say to our partner, "this is where the doctor will deliver your baby," we can immediately see how a simple sentence takes power *away* from our partner in birthing her baby. The entire process isn't even about *her* giving birth anymore – it's about the doctor "carrying the baton to the finish line." In that way, the language we use is essential not only to our partners, but to our own psychology in preparing ourselves for birth, and fatherhood.

Throughout this process you're going to hear from friends, relatives, doctors, and just about everyone else, as they give you their own two cents on birth. They're going to reiterate some things we've already mentioned: *childbirth = painful*, "delivery" rooms, even simple words like "labor" or common phrases like "failure to progress"; or further, a viewpoint of the entire birthing process not as "natural" or "physiological" but as prone to "risk," "intervention," and "emergencies."

We aren't trying to fundamentally change how you speak about birth, but we want to encourage you to be conscious of what you're saying and empathetic to how it comes across. The language of birth, just like the lasting effects of the outdated "alpha male" or the obstetrical "dilemma," on to "Twilight Sleep" and "delivery," all impact how we as birth partners think about birth. What we say out loud starts to fuel how we feel inside.

When we don't share our doubts or thoughts with our partners, but instead bottle them up only to express something negative later on when we can't keep it to ourselves any longer – we not only hurt them, but ourselves. In pregnancy, birth, and parenthood, taking on the challenges as a team influences how every stage pans out. It's okay to have doubts. It's okay to ask questions. It's okay to feel overwhelmed, anxious, or tired. Your role is to support your partner and yourself, not to be Superman. You don't have to be in a long-term committed relationship or married to your partner to do that, or for you both to be engaged and loving parents. You just have to decide to. It's not an easy thing to do, but it becomes easier when we acknowledge that our words impact our perspective.

Hypnobirthing is the body and mind of birth. That definition is usually in reference to your partner, but it also applies to you. Your role in hypnobirthing brings into account the old adage: "where the mind goes, the body follows." We want your body to follow your mind on a path to a positive birth experience. To do that, we're going to explore what makes a positive birth and the real steps you can take as a team to make it happen, together.

"Part of me was like - I don't really know what this is. But another part of me was just kind of unsure about how it was going to work and, you know, if we were going to get there and there was just going to be a clock swinging or a spoon being bent or something like that, which self-evidently there wasn't! But then another really big chunk of it was, you know, my partner really believes in this, so I do too. I think that is the absolute central pillar to it. The whole idea of Hypnobirthing is about buying into the same idea, whether you're the father or the mother. I think that's really important."

- Peter R. Newbury, UK.

"Even from the first session, Demelza (our Hypnobirthing instructor) laid out a plan and it really opened my eyes - everything from the process her body goes through to give birth - which was very cool - through to a physical representation of what was going to happen. It started to all make sense."

- Lewis J. Somerset, UK.

"When I started reading about hypnobirthing, it felt like something that we could both be involved in, and that would enable me to support Clemmie better than maybe I had done previously in other births."

- Simon H. Bristol, UK.

"When my wife decided we should go to talk to a hypnobirthing practitioner, I had never heard of it as a practice and had no idea why I was invited. At high school – like many people of my age group – I was obliged during sex education classes to watch a video of a traditional labour and birth. There was a lot of screaming, a lot of blood, and in retrospect I think that the video was actually intended to have contraceptive purposes for teenagers. It certainly didn't portray birth as a positive experience, and I don't seem to remember the dad actually being present. We went along for a talk, the practitioner explained that the dad was an integral part of the hypnobirthing process!"

- Simon F, Scotland, UK.

"I was very skeptical because I didn't know enough about it. I remember doing the first taster session, and Becky and I thought it was different, but we came away from it really relaxed and wanting more. It gave us more control and something we could work on together. The more we learnt about it the more we learnt it was about empowerment."

- Adam W. Royal Leamington Spa, UK.

CHAPTER TWO

CRAFTING THE CHAIR OF POSITIVE BIRTH

WHAT YOU'RE GOING TO LEARN:

- What a positive birth means to you right now
- How to craft the "Chair of Positive Birth"
- The science behind what is happening in the birth process
- Some common interventions in the birth process
- How to maintain the "Chair of Positive Birth"

In order to visualize your own path to positive birth, we want to offer this short exercise to see just what that phrase means for you *right now*. This isn't quite crafting a birth plan just yet, but it outlines the five most important aspects of what you feel a positive birth experience is for you – and to see just how aligned your partner is in their own view of this shared experience.

Below you'll see five sections broken up into the birth *process, bonding, method, location,* and *environment*. Beneath each, you'll see a set of options. Don't worry, it's not expected that you know in detail yet what each of the aspects of each section means. You will by the end of this book, but right now all you need to do is circle or mark one option in each section you see at this moment as the most important. Admittedly, it can be a difficult decision, as you may see multiple aspects in any given section that you definitely want, but try your best to only choose the *one* most important to you.

After you choose your own, get your partner to do the same on the identical checklist beside it and then compare with one another. There are no right answers, but what this checklist often does is start or refine those conversations about the decisions you'll both need to make early on. It's also good to have them written out, because what you might find is that certain choices may change as you further explore hypnobirthing and get closer to the big day.

PROCESS:

The process of birth that your partner would prefer to experience.

☐ ☐ No coached pushing

☐ ☐ Chosen birth positions

☐ ☐ Medicated (epidural & others)

☐ ☐ Unmedicated (natural birth)

BONDING:

The bonding practice with your baby that you and your partner hope to experience.

☐ ☐ Golden hour

☐ ☐ Delayed cord clamping

☐ ☐ Cutting the cord

METHOD:

The method of birth your partner chooses to have; this can also include the varieties of planned inductions, or water birth.

☐ ☐ Vaginal delivery (or VBAC)

☐ ☐ Caesarean birth

LOCATION:

The location where you and your partner would like to give birth.

☐ ☐ Birth at hospital

☐ ☐ Birth at home

☐ ☐ Birth at birthing center

ENVIRONMENT:

The birthing environment in regards to atmosphere, ambience, and those instruments or people involved that you and your partner would prefer to experience.

☐ ☐ Personalized atmosphere (lights, music, etc.)

☐ ☐ You or chosen others present in the room

☐ ☐ Fetal monitoring (continuous, intermittent, or none)

☐ ☐ No observed birth

SCORECARD + REFLECTIONS

- **5 out 5** - On the same page, it's like one mind!
  You and your partner are already highly in tune for your birth plan, but don't let it stop there. Take the next steps to ensure you're aligned on the birth itself too.
- **3-4 out of 5** - A chapter behind, but getting there.
  You and your partner have a good feel of where the other one is at when it comes to your birth plan, and over the next few chapters you'll both be ready for the big event.
- **1-2 out of 5** - Slighlly different pages, but that's ok, there's time! You and your partner fall into the majority of parents leading up to birth, where these conversations are new and unfamiliar. Don't be alarmed - there's lots of great learning ahead.

THE CHAIR OF POSITIVE BIRTH

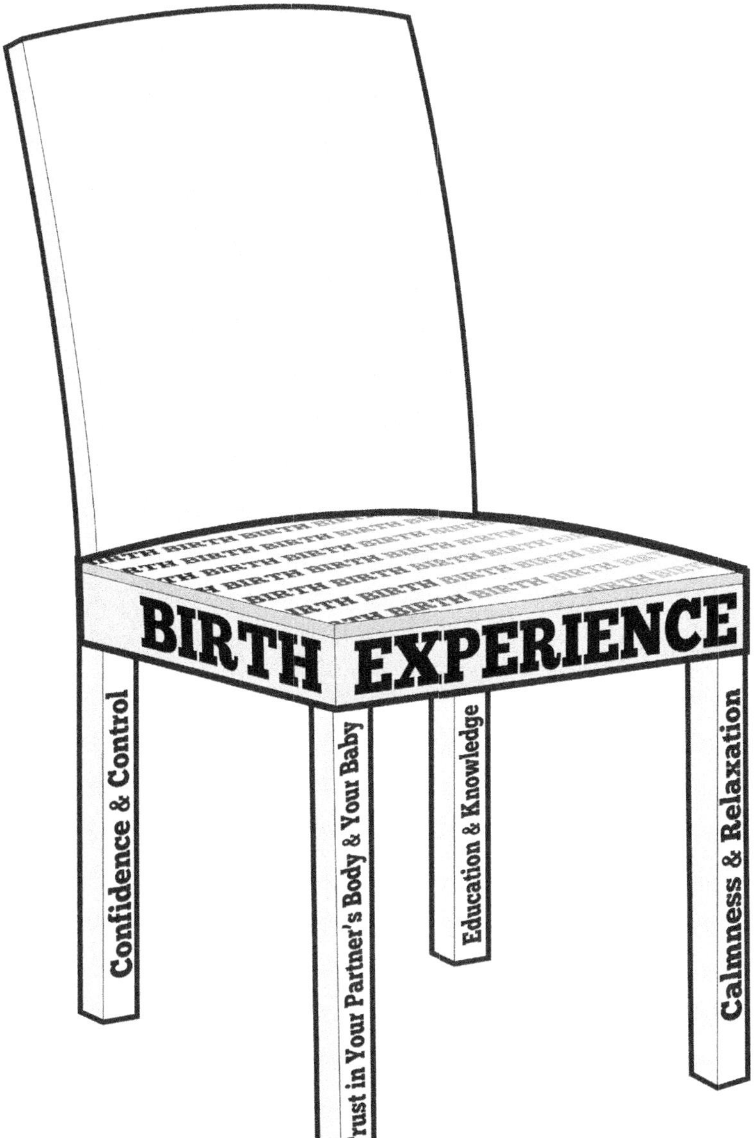

Whatever your feelings on birth right now, there will always be things we can't plan for and unforeseen problems that we can't account for. To help you further understand what helps lead to a positive birthing experience, we like to imagine the whole thing as a **chair**.

There are four legs on the chair that hold up the seat of hypnobirthing.

To have a successful positive birth, your partner has to sit comfortably on this chair that you help to construct.

THE FIRST LEG: TRUST IN YOUR PARTNER'S BODY & YOUR BABY

The first leg of hypnobirthing and the path to positive birth is trust. Trust that your partner's body and your baby know how to do this. It's extremely common for new mothers to feel like they don't know what to expect and won't know what to do when the time comes.

Let them know, *they will*.

Hypnobirthing teaches them and you that birth is a completely natural process and their bodies are equipped for it. Everything about their reproductive physiology is designed to facilitate labor and birth. Thousands of years of evolution means that your partner and your baby (or, you know, humanity) are quite literally *made* for this.

The key to this trust however, is an inversion of expectations.

With the advances of modern medicine, we've come to be conditioned to see birth as a medical process, with natural tendencies and instincts getting in the way of safety. Instead, hypnobirthing teaches that birth is a completely natural process, one that only sometimes requires medical intervention.

By first understanding how this natural process works, you can see how things are meant to progress, and better understand anything that is slowing or preventing that progression. Knowing what *should* happen will help you and your partner know if something is actually wrong and if interventions are necessary. To outline how this process works, we're going to take a look at the science behind the uterus, the cervix, the pelvis, and the four most important hormones in birth to see how they all work together. First up:

THE UTERUS

The uterus or the "womb" is, first and foremost, a muscle. Specifically, it is two layers of banded muscles, both vertical and horizontal, that are shaped like an upside-down pear and work together during labor to open up the cervix and push the baby out.

When left to its own devices, the uterus is really good at doing that.

An average woman who has never been pregnant has a uterus that measures about 7 centimeters in length. During pregnancy, the uterus stretches almost 500 times that size to become the baby's home for nine months. As the baby gets bigger, the uterus has to get bigger too. Even more impressive, after the birth, it shrinks back down again, close to its original size, averaging about 9 centimeters rather than 7.

The big job of the uterus is *contracting* to push the baby down and out. In the first stage of labor, your partner's contractions will begin to encourage the baby with gentle nudges to "get out, please ."Many hypnobirthing experts call these contractions, *surges.* Before the big day, the uterus prepares itself, your partner, and the baby for what these surges might feel like through Braxton Hicks contractions or "false labor" contractions.

The surge is said to feel like a wave. During labor, many midwives and hypnobirthing experts use the expression "ride the wave." As in, they tell your partner to mentally ride through this surge of the uterus, focusing on the feeling, as they prepare for the next one. The wave is the feeling of the uterus pushing downward, which is the vertical outer layer (myometrium) drawing up like window blinds, and the inner horizontal layer (endometrium) staying soft and relaxed as they bundle together. The closer to the birth of your baby, the more frequent and more powerful these surges become.

The combination of these movements helps guide the baby downward, as their head puts pressure on the cervix to open up (that's how you get to that "10 cm dilated" you might have heard about in every sitcom ever).

Which brings us to...

THE CERVIX

If you think of the uterus like an upside-down pear then the cervix is the stem on top (bottom?). The cervix is another muscular channel that connects the uterus (above) and the vagina (below). The cervix is basically the middle of the "birth canal" that everyone has been talking about.

The cervix already played a huge role during conception leading the sperm to the ovaries, getting this whole thing underway. However, up until labor begins, it is also clogged up with *cervical mucus* – a thick layer that develops early in the first trimester to stop germs, bacteria, viruses, or more sperm from entering the uterus.

During labor, the cervix's job changes. Because of that, let's go ahead and change the analogy – the cervix is no longer the stem of a pear, it's the tie at the bottom of a water balloon. The cervical mucus had this water balloon tied (clogged) uptight, with nothing going in or out, but now it's opening, ever so slightly, in preparation for the birth.

FIBRONECTIN FUN FACT:

Fibronectin is a protein that the baby uses to tell us that they're done growing. When the baby has reached what they have decided to be their birthing size, they'll release the protein called fibronectin into the amniotic sac. This protein makes its way to the cervix. The cervix registers this protein, which basically tells it to "start getting ready for the birth" because "the baby is on their way down." Fibronectin is also what doctors can check for in vaginal fluid to see how close to labor your partner might be. If there's no fibronectin, labor is likely still a couple of weeks away. If there is fibronectin, get yourself ready because labor is imminent!

During the first stage of labor, the muscular layers of the uterus gently nudge the baby to "get out, please" through contractions, and the cervix starts to open to let the baby out. The process of opening is called *effacement* or *ripening*. The cervix starts out long, firm, and narrow – but as labor progresses, it shortens, softens, and widens. As it begins to do that, you may see a clear-ish, pinkish, or bloody discharge sometimes called the "bloody show."

This is the release of that mucus plug that formed in the first trimester.

So, as this process unfolds, the cervix is doing two things: thinning (effacing) and opening (dilating). The common indicator that the second stage of labor has begun is when the cervix is 10 centimeters dilated and around 100% effaced. After that, with the help of the uterus, the cervix pushes the baby down and out through the vagina. However, to make room for all that to happen, we look to:

THE PELVIS

We've talked about the major muscles used in birth, but what about the bones?

The pelvis (which has a bunch of cool names like *pelvic girdle* or *bony pelvis*) is a basin-shaped complex of bones located above the thighs and below the abdomen. In most all humans, the pelvis supports our spine, protects our organs, and holds us upright so that we can stand, walk, and run. Where women are slightly different in preparation for childbirth is that they have a wider, more rounded pelvis with thinner bones to help make it easier for a baby to pass through.

The pelvis is comprised of two main parts:

- Sacrum – spade-shaped bone, formed by the fusion of 5 separate vertebrae
- Coccyx – the tail bone, formed by the fusion of 4 separate bones

And three hip bones:

- Ilium – the broad, jutting portion of the hip bone at the crest of the pelvis
- Pubis – the lower, back side of the hip bone
- Ischium – the curved bone that helps to form the hip

All of these together are vital to childbirth, but the two we're going to focus on are the sacrum and the coccyx. The pelvic floor muscles connect these two parts of the pelvis to form a sort of sling. This holds the weight of the growing uterus, baby, and everything else in place during pregnancy.

Often at around 36 weeks, the baby starts to drop a little lower into the pelvis in a process called *lightening*, and this is a pretty clear sign that the body is about to begin preparing for labor. However, keep in mind that the preparation process could still go on for weeks.

During that time, your partner's body will begin to secrete hormones (which we'll get into soon) that soften the ligaments of the pelvis, allowing it to open up for the baby to travel through. The pelvic floor muscles then spread apart during contractions, allowing the baby to make their way through the cervix a little easier.

More than just the muscles, the sacrum and the coccyx actually open up themselves too. Assuming the mother isn't lying on her back, the sacrum can actually be observed opening up. It moves backward during the second stage of labor (the "pushing" stage) and increases the diameter of the pelvis, letting the baby have just a little extra space to maneuver. This is called "the opening of the back," and the reason it isn't talked about very often (and honestly looks so wild to see firsthand) is because the traditional birth method still has women lying on their back for delivery.

When lying on their back, the sacrum is unable to open up the pelvis naturally, making the birth canal narrower, which can both prolong the labor and increase the likelihood of severe stretching or tearing. With that in mind, all these muscles and bones work naturally together to make childbirth as smooth a process as possible. But they would still be nothing without the complex mixture of hormones that facilitate all of it:

THE BIG FOUR HORMONES

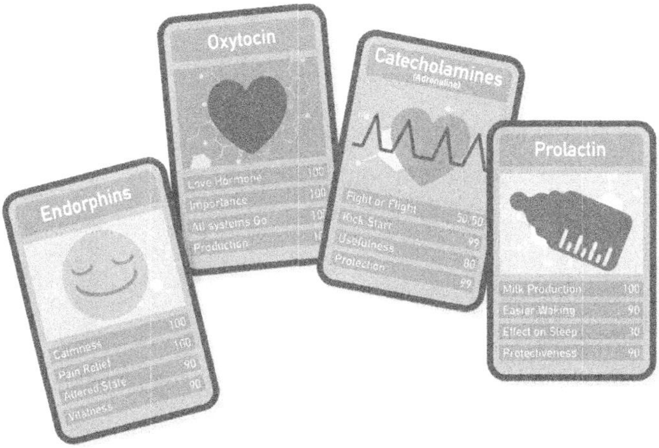

The right balance of hormones is essential for a successful pregnancy. Hormones are the body's chemical messengers that carry information between the brain and the muscles, tissues, organs, and pretty much everything else. Hormones most often travel by blood, and there are a ton involved in ensuring the birth process is as smooth and safe as possible. During labor and birth, they guide your partner on how to:

- Prepare the body for birth
- Begin contractions
- Prepare the breasts to make milk to provide sustenance for the baby
- Prepare the baby for life outside of the womb

The four most significant hormones involved are oxytocin, catecholamines (adrenaline), prolactin, and endorphins. We've already talked a good amount about oxytocin and adrenaline, however, to emphasize just how crucial a role they all play, we're going to outline a few extra important points about each.

OXYTOCIN

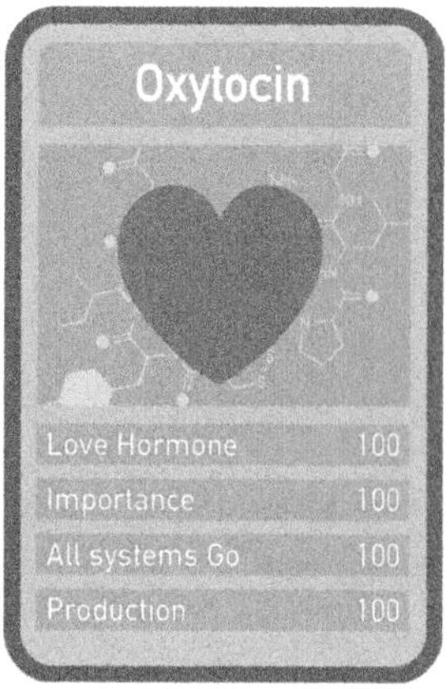

The "love" hormone.

Arguably the most important hormone because it gets the whole labor process started.

Once the baby's brain is developed, it sends out oxytocin to say "I'm ready to be born now," and then your partner's uterus picks up on that signal and begins their own oxytocin production. All systems go!

FUN FACT:

After the birth, we as birth partners and dads also produce oxytocin when we hold, cuddle, or simply play with our babies. The increased production actually encourages us to more easily bond with our baby. In that way, it's a vital part of the "Golden Hour" and "skin-to-skin" for mom and for you – but we'll go into more detail on that later.

CATECHOLAMINES (ADRENALINE)

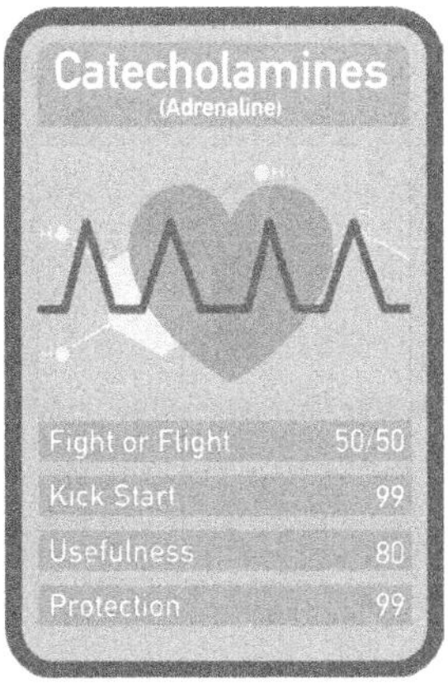

The "fight or flight" hormones.

We said that we were trying to dissuade the encouragement of adrenaline, but right at the beginning of labor, after the baby tells your partner that it's go time, a surge of adrenaline actually helps kick-start the whole process.

It's during labor that a little too much adrenaline is going to start to push the oxytocin production down. That's why it's your goal to limit fear, anxiety, and stress during labor and encourage confidence, calm, and control.

"I was surprised to learn that adrenaline was something to avoid during birth. I thought of adrenaline as something that drives you on in most situations. When you have an adrenaline rush it boosts you, doesn't it? Learning that this is the opposite of what you want in birth was a surprise. Obviously the science behind that made sense. If you were giving birth in the wild and a lion comes along, you need to stop what you're doing and run away. That's why adrenaline has that effect. It slows down the birth because then an animal that is under threat mid-birth can flee rather than continuing to give birth and getting eaten. It was a surprise but it made perfect sense too!"

- Adam R. Brighton, UK.

ENDORPHINS

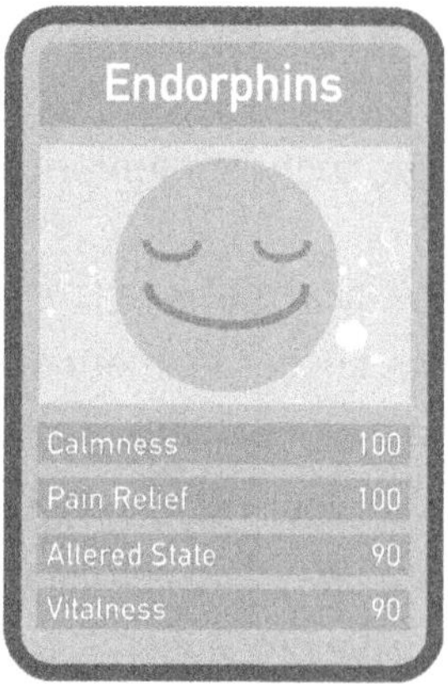

The "calm" and "pain-relieving" hormones.

When you face stress or pain (like working out), your body releases endorphins. If enough are released, like during a marathon or labor, they can actually propel the mind to an altered state of consciousness which makes it easier for runners to "push past the wall" or women to better cope with the birth process.

During labor, women who don't receive medication will have their endorphins steadily rise, just like running a marathon. However, pain medications like morphine or an epidural, can cause a steep drop in natural endorphins. This is likely because the medicine is taking over the job of the hormones.

Fun Fact: Babies also produce endorphins during birth to help them better cope with the process, stay calm, and relieve pain. That's vital, especially as the skull is compressed, in a manner of speaking, (more so that it's made up of bones that haven't fused together making it more malleable) to move through the birth canal.

PROLACTIN

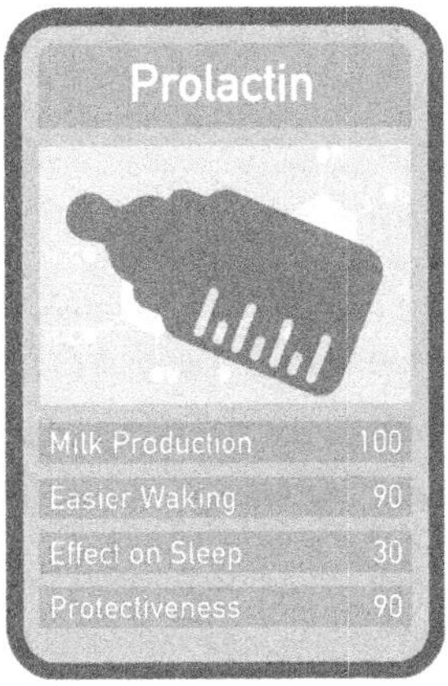

The hormone responsible for breast milk production.

While it is most known for lactation, it also helps mothers to wake easier to help them be more immediately attentive to their baby – but the drawback is that it makes sleep in the third trimester more difficult.

During labor, prolactin and its effect on sleep is vital. Labor can be a very long process, one as, or more, difficult than running a marathon, and your partner is likely to get extremely exhausted. Prolactin, alongside endorphins, allows her body to take the most effective naps of her entire life. Some women have claimed that a nap that only lasted thirty seconds felt like hours!

THE SECOND LEG: CALMNESS & RELAXATION

Hypnobirthing holds many meditative practices at the core of its philosophy. These practices empower your partner to be calm and relaxed throughout labor and birth. Although it takes practice, repetition, and a lot of tools in your birth partner's toolbelt, encouraging your partner to remain calm and relaxed is essential to the natural production of oxytocin, which (we know we sound like a broken record by now) helps the uterus to contract and progress labor. However, this leg is also a reason why hypnobirthing is so often linked with quicker labor – if we can limit the stressors and remain calm, the body will tell the baby that it's safe to arrive.

Hypnobirthing tools that relax us can also enable us to switch off our neocortex, to "quiet" our minds. The neocortex is the thinking part of the brain, and it's active when we're talking, thinking, and making everyday decisions. For example, if the neocortex is active when the barista says, "enjoy your coffee," you might respond with "thank you." If it's not active, or you're distracted, you might immediately blurt out, "you too!" instead. Yeah, that's the worst. If the neocortex is stimulated during labor, your partner's body is far more likely to produce adrenaline. Conversely, when this part of our brain is quiet – when constant anxieties or stressors aren't circling like a carousel – the other parts of the brain are free to take over. The complex combination of hormones are free to do what they need to do for labor to happen instinctively.

To reduce the likelihood of adrenaline production ramping up, or to stop it almost entirely, hypnobirthing teaches a host of scripts, breathing techniques, and visualization techniques that enable your partner to reach that sought-after state of calmness and relaxation – and very importantly, stay there.

In the next chapter, we outline all of those techniques and how to incorporate them to encourage a positive birth experience.

"The course that we did, in particular was focused quite heavily initially on the science behind the hormones and how they impact birth. So before we even started thinking about breathing or positive affirmations, all of these things that we did very much embrace, it was more about understanding why they would be effective. So learning about adrenaline, learning about how that would be something that is not going to help on the day and learning about oxytocin and how you want to be trying to drive those levels up to try and make the birth smoother and all that stuff. I remember that being the thing that was the wake up moment - knowing the science behind the techniques and why they're important, then it meant we could jump in and grasp the techniques a bit more."

- Adam R. Brighton, UK.

THE THIRD LEG: EDUCATION & KNOWLEDGE

Mindfulness and relaxation are often seen as the core of hypnobirthing, but they would be nothing without knowledge and understanding of how the woman's body works during pregnancy, labor, and birth. We've gone over the various parts of a woman's body and how they all work together during the natural process of birth, but now it's important to look at the things that can affect that process.

The education and knowledge leg arms (ha, leg arms) mothers and dads-to-be with all the information they need to ensure you both can make the best, most informed decisions for your partner and the baby during the birth process.

It helps to encourage using logic and understanding to approach any decision or intervention that may arise during labor, such as the use of Pitocin or receiving an induction, an epidural, or a cervical examination. It also outlines what "failure to progress" actually means. We're about to go over each of those (*epidurals* will be covered in the Birth Chapter), but it's important to know, before we do, that women aren't required by law to accept any medical procedure or examination during pregnancy or labor, even down to an internal examination. Although saying "no" can be difficult, especially when you're in certain situations and things are made to seem dire, it's essential to be confident of your own boundaries, beliefs, and stances.

That being said, it is also vital to be aware that *any* medical professional you deal with should be asking your partner for consent before acting on *any* procedure, as with anything in life that regards a woman's body.

INDUCTION

An induction is a way for doctors to artificially encourage uterine contractions to kick-start labor and achieve a vaginal birth. Most commonly, they do so by administering Pitocin (or similar synthetic oxytocin).

Often, an induction is recommended for medical reasons to reduce the risk of complications to the mother or the baby. These risks may include high blood pressure, pre-eclampsia, fetal growth restrictions, or any other potential problem outlined by a medical professional. When used for medical reasons, an induction can be an extremely safe and effective way to a healthy birth. However, it is essential to know that although the methods doctors use to induce labor are extensive, your partner's body still has to accept the jump start to get everything going. Resistance to the induction, or starting it early, can result in an extremely long labor.

With that in mind, a popular trend now is elective inductions. This is where pregnant women and their partners choose a date of induction so that they can better plan when their baby is born. However, it is important to know that elective inductions sow the seed that your partner will *not* be able to birth without an induction.

There are medical reasons for elective inductions too, but if it's something you're both considering, just keep in mind that although you are *choosing* the date of birth, it still might not go exactly according to plan. Some elective inductions have resulted in labors lasting well over a day and if the induction fails a caesarean birth is the likely alternative solution to ensure the safety of the mother and baby.

"It wasn't until Hypnobirthing that we felt kind of educated about this stuff. And we felt like we had more knowledge to negotiate these situations. We definitely would have been more just following the doctor's advice and doing what we're told, but actually there were times when she was recommended an induction after we had done the Hypnobirthing class. And during our birthing we had learned about induction, and that it's there for a purpose, and should be used if it's absolutely needed. And of course, it's there in situations where it can really help, but it shouldn't be just done as a standard protocol. My partner had some issues with movement and not being able to feel the baby towards the end. So we went to the hospital a few times just to check things over. And because we had gone maybe like three or four times, we spoke to an obstetrician and he said 'I would strongly suggest that you have an induction and I can book it in' - just like that. As we had done the Hypnobirthing, we knew that this could introduce complications or more kinds of unpleasant birth experiences. So she actually went against the advice and that really shocked me. I was 100% thinking whatever he says she's just going to do it because he's a trained medical professional guy, but she knew her body and her rights. But it really did shock me that she was like, No, I'm just going to hang on because, you know, I don't want to take those risks unnecessarily."

- Jitender S. Brighton, UK.

CERVICAL CHECK

A cervical check is where a doctor or midwife puts their gloved fingers into your partner's vagina to check effacement and dilation. This is a way to see how the labor is progressing. The medical professional can use this information to make adjustments to Pitocin levels or give a better estimate as to when the next stage of labor, the pushing stage, will likely begin.

The numbers most doctors are looking for are 10 cm dilated and nearly 100% effaced. It should be noted however, that the process of dilation and effacement can happen in almost any timeframe. Some women will move from 4cm to 10cm dilation in hours, and some will do the same in minutes. As we mentioned, all bodies are different, and all labor is too. Even so, if a doctor does perform a cervical check on your partner, they should always ask for consent before doing so.

It may seem like a routine procedure, and it often is, but it's always important to remember the very real implications of a lack of consent for something so personal.

BREAKING OF THE WATERS

"Breaking of the waters" is an older phrase that actually means the rupture of the amniotic sac - the thin membrane that houses the baby and stores all that remarkable amniotic fluid within the uterus.

You know in those movies and TV shows when the pregnant woman yells out (at an inopportune moment), "My water just broke!" That's what this is, but the rupture of the sac doesn't mean you have to speed to the hospital, birthing center, or wherever the birth is happening. In most pregnancies, the amniotic sac will rupture naturally, and it's a tell-tale sign that the baby is on the way - but not here just yet.

However, in the event of an induction, one way to encourage the labor to progress is through a "breaking of the waters." To artificially break the waters, a doctor or midwife will often use a small hook and apply pressure to encourage the sac to release the waters. This often allows the baby's head to put more pressure on the cervix, speeding the labor along. The most important thing to remember about the breaking of the waters, other than what we've covered in the induction section, is that it also often puts an artificial timer on the birth.

Most hospitals and some midwives won't allow labor to go more than 12 hours after the water breaks to ensure the safety of the baby, who has lost somewhat of a safety cushion within the uterus as contractions bear down on them. If labor does not progress at that pace, another intervention might result from the popular phrase:

"FAILURE TO PROGRESS"

A majority of hypnobirthing practices are created to make the labor and birth process as fast, smooth, safe, and empowering as possible. However, that isn't always the case. All women's bodies are different, and labor can progress in different ways. If that progression isn't in line or on target with a doctor's predetermined parameters, they're more likely to intervene in the process to "speed it up."

As we've mentioned before, fear in the birthing room, stress, anxiety, or any possible complication can cause the labor to slow down. This can be an issue as more prolonged labor can pose greater risks to the well-being of the mother and baby. That being said, long labors aren't inherently a sign of danger or a medical emergency. Sometimes, the natural rhythm between the baby and the mother just happens to cause a more prolonged labor, and that's okay.

With that in mind, a "failure to progress" is one of the most commonly heard phrases used by doctors before they intervene or opt for an emergency caesarean birth. The problem with that, as we'll outline more in the Birth section, is that many birthing environments aren't conducive to feelings of calm, relaxation, confidence, and control. Because of that, a "failure to progress" is something you're actively trying to avoid. If a caesarean birth isn't part of your birth plan and isn't what you both had in mind as part of your positive birth experience, then having one thrust upon your partner can be traumatic – even if it is necessary.

With every decision, it is not only important but also empowering for both you and your partner to know the benefits, risks, and alternatives. This can help you to come to the best solutions for you, them, their body, their birth, and your baby.

THE FOURTH LEG: CONFIDENCE & CONTROL

The last leg of hypnobirthing helps the woman have confidence and control over her mind and her body – **confidence** in her ability to make informed decisions, and **control** in her ability to give birth in a positive way.

A lack of confidence during birth can cause a lot of undue stress, starting that vicious cycle of adrenaline production and prolonged labor. Whether from a woman's voice not being heard, her desires not being acknowledged, or anything else, the feeling of being out of control is something that a lot of women fear heading into labor. That's why an important leg of hypnobirthing is women feeling confident and in control of any situation that may arise during the birthing process.

The way that you can help your partner to feel confident and in control of their birth experience is by knowing what they want that experience to look like in the first place. To do that, it's all about preparation. In the fourth chapter, "Before the Birth," we're going to go into detail about everything you need to know to prepare for the birth, including where you would both like to give birth, who will be involved, what you need to bring, how you can create a positive birth environment, and perhaps most importantly, how to design your very own *Birth Plan*.

PUTTING IT ALL TOGETHER

With all those legs intact, the foundation of hypnobirthing is formed. At times the chair may get a little wobbly, your partner may lose some calmness or trust in her own body and she may lose confidence in what she's doing or feel out of control. However, that's where you come in. In addition to being the Guardian, you're also the one who repairs that chair before, during, and after the birth.

In order to do that, you need to know your stuff.

You need to know which leg needs sanding, which one needs a fresh stain, or which leg is a little short and is causing the chair to be off-balance. You need to know when a bolt-on one leg needs tightening or when to add a foot on another to keep it from slipping.

Your role is to keep that chair in working order so that your partner can focus all their energy on listening to their body during labor and birth. Because to experience a positive birth, first and foremost and regardless of your relationship, you need each other. Remember, you're a team in all of this.

Now, let's get you the right toolset for the job.

"My wife was really the catalyst for starting the hypnobirthing classes and you have to know, it may seem rare nowadays, but this was almost a decade ago now. She had discovered these practices, read the books, and wanted to hire a personal hypnobirthing expert. I was extremely skeptical at first, but three children later, we've practiced hypnobirthing in every birth, and my wife is actually pursuing an education right now to practice hypnobirthing herself! Safe to say its become an integral part of our lives."

- Phil L. North Oxfordshire, UK.

"I really was impressed with the idea of Hypnobirthing . As someone who has probably always struggled a bit with anxiety, I liked the idea of using imagery and calming techniques to center the mind in a time of distress."

- Aaron K. New York, US.

"I found it to be really quite liberating - knowing that there was another way to view birth. It was just the fact that Hypnobirthing is trying to make birthing natural again. And although medicine has a place in all this since birth does not always go as smoothly as we would always want it to. It's just a much more balanced approach."

- Piers C. Bristol, UK.

> "I was raised in a much more traditional medicated hospital kind of environment. You know, epidurals were normal. Birth was seen as like this scary, dangerous thing. But as I began learning with Jessica, I realised natural birth wasn't just like a hippie thing. That actually this is the most normal human natural thing you can experience as a woman because your body's made for it!"
>
> - Ben L. Arkansas, US.

> "It was really important for me to help get Katrina into an environment where she felt confident, calm, and ready for what she's going to do and to be excited about it. I think it was really pivotal for me to buy into that because otherwise the whole process isn't going to work. So I think that's the key thing, which I've tried to reinforce in my own mind since I learned the skills. Those skills are based around breathing techniques, relaxation techniques, and being able to deal with stressful situations by calming your body down."
>
> - Peter R. Newbury, UK

CHAPTER THREE

THE POSITIVE BIRTH PARTNER TOOLSET

WHAT YOU'RE GOING TO LEARN:

The tools of hypnobirthing taught by a hypnobirthing expert including:

- Breathing techniques
- Relaxation scripts
- Setting anchors
- B.R.A.I.N. – Benefits, Risks, Alternatives, Instincts, Nothing
- Creating the right environment
- Continuity of care

Now that you have the philosophy and science of hypnobirthing down, it's time to give you the tools that will help you put them into action. Hypnobirthing, beyond the study of positive birth, is a set of techniques meant to make that positive birth a reality. We call it the *positive birth partner toolset* because that's precisely what it is. This is your kit filled to the brim with all the tools you might need to use during labor and birth.

However, until you find yourself in that moment, you won't know exactly which tool you'll need – but that's the whole idea. This toolset is you being prepared for *anything.* You'll have every possible tool at your disposal. You may not need to use every single one in your set, but you will have them all just in case.

In this chapter, we're going to outline those tools to fill your set. To do that in the best way possible, we've enlisted the help of a real hypnobirthing expert, Natalie Reed, to help us. She is the founder of Birthing Matters (www.birthing-matters.com) and across her years of experience and study, she has outlined for us the very best tools that you, as a birth partner, will learn alongside your partner. You'll learn how these tools can benefit your partner when it comes to labor and birth, and how you, too, can use these tools to not only support them through the labor process, but to also support yourself!

So, let's start with the first tool in your set:

BREATHING TECHNIQUES

Are you actually going to be taught *how* to breathe?
In a nutshell, yeah – pretty much.

We know you already know how to do this (and that nobody has used "mouth-breather" as an insult since the 90s), but do you know how to effectively incorporate breathing when it comes to labor to help you and your partner to feel calm, focused, and relaxed? Let's break that down a little more...

There are two types of breathing techniques that hypnobirthing focuses on:

UP BREATHING AND DOWN BREATHING

Down breathing is really for your partner – it's the technique they call upon in the final stage of labor when they feel their muscles bearing downward. That's why it's called "down breathing ."The baby is moving *down* their birth canal and the breathing technique focuses on your partner breathing *down* their body. When they feel the start of a contraction or surge, they take a quick, deep breath in through their nose and on the exhale they send the breath *down* their body.

Now, up breathing, on the other hand – that can be for you as well as your partner.

In the early stages of labor, onward to established labor (don't worry, we're going to go over every stage in detail in the *Birth* chapter), the uterine muscles are working hard drawing upwards and outwards. This helps dilate the cervix and move the baby down. What we want to do at this stage is mimic that motion. We want your breathing and your partner's breathing to emulate what their body is doing.

Up breathing involves taking a nice, slow breath in through the nose, and a long, slow, warm breath out through the mouth. Your out-breath will be slightly longer, and (pro-tip) it's on this out-breath that the hormone oxytocin is produced. Sometimes, when your partner has all those distractions, you reminding her of that simple, in—up—out pattern can help her to regain her center and continue on with that vital production of oxytocin. To add to that, continued and consistent oxytocin production is what's needed to fuel labor and keep the surges coming at a steadier rate.

To that end, by exhaling longer on the out-breath, your partner's mind and body will feel relaxed and calm, and that'll tell their body it doesn't need to produce adrenaline because they're not in any danger and don't need their "fight or flight" response. Instead, it sends signals that they're safe and relaxed – so it can keep right on producing oxytocin. As a quick reminder, in labor, we don't want oxygen and blood sent to the extremities because the goal is to have it focused on the uterus and the baby's path to birth. There's no lion or fire-breathing dragon in the room with you, your partner is safe, and your goal is to embody that feeling as well so that we can keep things calm and relaxed. Limiting adrenaline means oxytocin can work its magic, and up-breathing is a really great tool for doing this.

Sounds great for the person in labor, doesn't it? But you'll also reap the benefits with this technique of breathing, because labor really can go on for a long time. This type of breathing helps you to stay calm, feel relaxed, and conserve energy during that possibly sleepless night after your full week of work. Sure, you're not the one giving birth, but you're still there by her side for the duration and keeping your energy levels in check to help you and your partner stay focused and calm is a big plus.

To further emphasize, if you're using up breathing, your partner will tend to copy you too. You're there to support and prompt them; a gentle, soft-voiced reminder can work but we want to limit any disturbances or conversations so they can focus all their energy on their labor. Because of that, using up breathing yourself to prompt them or along with them is a great way to be there for them in the moment.

In that way, just as your partner might be practicing her breathing techniques during pregnancy, you can too. Any time during your day is fine, but you'll see the greatest benefit when put to practice during a time or moment when you feel particularly anxious, worried, or generally a bit on-edge. Maybe you have a meeting you're nervous about, a job interview, an appointment, or you're even running late to meet a friend. Take a moment and practice your up breathing in those moments, focusing on your breaths in and up and out, and you'll begin to feel that wave of calm wash over you.

"Practising the breathing was really helpful in the build-up to the birth because all of these techniques made us feel confident that on the day, we were going in with as much information as possible. And I think that was the main thing for me, because obviously I wasn't able to give birth, so it was great knowing that I had all of these things up my sleeve if I needed them. It meant I felt I could have as much of an influence over proceedings as possible, in terms of not influencing perhaps, but being able to help Claire on the day."

- Adam R. Brighton, UK.

"We had a couple of different visualisations that she used for breathing. So similar to the thought of balloons and creating the technique to blow the balloons away and breathe, breathe, making it make the candle move or the petals on a flower move. So it was focusing on something and then breathing in line with that. It meant that when she was struggling, or when, you know, when I could see that she was in a bit of pain, or she was struggling a bit I could say what 'let's do the balloon one, or I'm going to put this track on.' And that's the track we use for that visualisation, or this is a track we use for that one. So it just meant I could be a bit more useful than just standing next to her just saying she's doing really well."

- John H, Hampshire, UK.

RELAXATION SCRIPTS

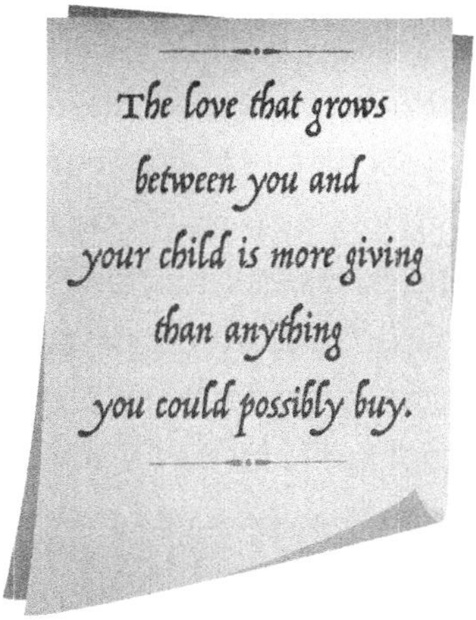

This tool actually goes hand-in-hand with the calmness and relaxation leg of our positive birth chair. Relaxation scripts that you, as a couple, will have access to and even create yourselves during pregnancy are there to be practiced, repeated, and used together. They are specifically designed and written to instill a deep state of relaxation in those who are listening to them. Relaxation scripts are used for all manner of things outside of birth, such as overcoming phobias or giving up a certain habit. They're not quite a mantra-like Thomas the Tank Engine saying, "I think I can, I think I can" – but they are simple stories that you can recite in full or in small part to evoke a positive emotion. Let's break that down further.

Relaxation scripts will start by using language and wording to relieve stress or anxiety from your partner, focusing on relaxing their entire body bit by bit, from head to toe. From there, they'll move on to the main portion of the script which tends to focus on imagery and vivid pictures; imagining yourself lying under a tree, or looking up at a sky full of clouds, with birds and butterflies flying around, a soft wind blowing, and a gentle stream trickling by, for example. The purpose being that she will use these mental images to hone in on what the script is specifically for, such as confidence towards birth, or letting go of fears.

The relaxation scripts that you'll be using are all geared towards birth and feeling positive, relaxed, and confident towards it. As the birth partner, you can have these scripts on hand and read them out loud to your partner throughout pregnancy – or you can memorize them. The key here is practicing them because your cadence, tone, and delivery are essential parts of their effectiveness. In that way, the goal is to start developing and using them during pregnancy so when it comes time for labor, that mind and body connection between the script itself and the feeling of being calm and confident is already second nature to your partner.

The more you practice together, the more your voice alone will become a trigger to relax for them too. It's all about strengthening what the mind takes in (your voice/the script's words) and how their body interprets and reacts (feeling calm, comforted, and confident). As with all the tools in hypnobirthing, practice is an important part in changing our mindset and approach, and this certainly isn't an exception.

You could even think about recording your voice reading the scripts, so your partner can listen to them when you're not there. When it comes time for labor, she may have certain scripts from all of those that you've used that she particularly likes and wants to use. Think of it like a mixtape back in the day, only with a lot more *you*. Or, you might find things are moving pretty quickly and there isn't time to read an entire script to her, or she doesn't actually want one. That's where the short relaxations can come in.

Short relaxations take triggers from entire scripts, and can be used in place of them. For example, one particular script may focus on the use of the word 'soften' throughout. It's the repetition of this word that will become recognized by your partner's mind. When she hears your voice in labor gently saying the word 'soften' to her, her mind will recognize it, and her body will react the way that it did when you practiced the relaxation in pregnancy – by feeling calm, soft, and comforted.

Don't forget you can download 110 example affirmations and relaxation scripts too at www.daddilife.com/hypnobirthingtoolkit

"I remember we stuck the positive affirmations up all over the house, which was quite funny because obviously every time you have friends over they're reading them and they're getting quite confused, asking why you've got these random phrases in the kitchen, bathroom and bedroom. And whilst they didn't necessarily help me as much, they were more for Claire to sort of get her in the zone."

- Adam R. Brighton, UK.

"I think what did it for me was realising the vulnerability that women feel leading up to childbirth, especially if they haven't been through it before. I think there was a phrase that, birth isn't something that's done to you. It's something that you do. And that was something that I heard more in Hypnobirthing rather than in NCT courses."

- Adam S. Tunbridge Wells, UK.

"I read the positive affirmations out quite a bit, too and we did a few of them. So we had our little book and when she practiced relaxing it was there to help guide us. There were the one or two stroke bumps and we definitely did a few of them. But at the same time, you don't necessarily go to them in the moment. So it would be good for learning to relax. And I think that's more for me learning to be relaxed whilst she was pregnant too!"

- Joe S. Tonbridge, UK.

SETTING ANCHORS

We've talked about breathing techniques and relaxation scripts, and now it's time for anchors. Anchors are used to trigger an automatic connection to a feeling, place, or moment, and you probably use them already without even noticing. If we asked you to think about your favorite holiday, can you now hear the sea lapping on the shore? Or smell the sunscreen or the warm evening air? Or when you smell your partner's perfume, can you remember when you first met? Anchors transport our mind to a place, memory, or feeling that's either real or imagined.

Smell, sight, sound, taste, and touch – our senses can all be anchors. Your partner might have some already that she wants to use during labor; maybe there's a smell or a song that evokes a happy memory for her. Did you ever notice in school that if you study with music on, when you take the test and hear the song, you'll remember the answers? The same sort of concept applies here. Only instead of just a song, we are able to cultivate an environment that engages and enlivens all of our senses.

We use anchors in hypnobirthing, every single one that we have available, because they are such powerful tools to encourage real feelings in the moment – to lock us firmly in place at sea no matter how choppy the waves are around us. With anchors set, we're safe.

Your role as birth partner is to have these anchors available when the time comes, whether it's hanging up photos of loved ones around the room, pinning twinkling lights from the walls behind her, putting on the playlist she's created, or placing essential oils on a warm cloth for her to smell. Talking with each other during pregnancy so you have an understanding of exactly which anchors she wants when she's in labor will mean that you're prepared to set these up and have them ready for her when the time comes.

"There were a couple of different tracks we used a lot. She downloaded them, it might have been on Spotify, that they were from, and there were different sort of talking tracks, with someone was talking through the breathing. And then there was different music that she found the best bit of music to work for this visualisation. So it ended up that every night she listened to that music, and it just naturally triggered us to do this breathing exercise to it. As soon as that bit of sound came on, straightaway, she knew it and fell into the breathing that she'd been doing, and by the end of the second trimester it was almost a habit.

- John H. Hampshire, UK.

"The Positive affirmations cards were fantastic to do. We were in lockdown so there was a limited amount we could do outside the home, but I'd leave one randomly by the kettle, or around her work. It gave her and me a boost, and was an important anchor for us."

- Lewis J. Somerset, UK.

"We were listening to a lot of different affirmations during our sessions with Holly, and after a couple of times she gave us these pre recorded ones, along with some music. And I don't know if this is a standard piece of music for Hypnobirthing, but we chose one that really connected with Rhian. It's a very gentle kind of piano melody that we ended up using solely when we were in in Hypnobirthing mode."

- Laurie A. London, UK.

B.R.A.I.N

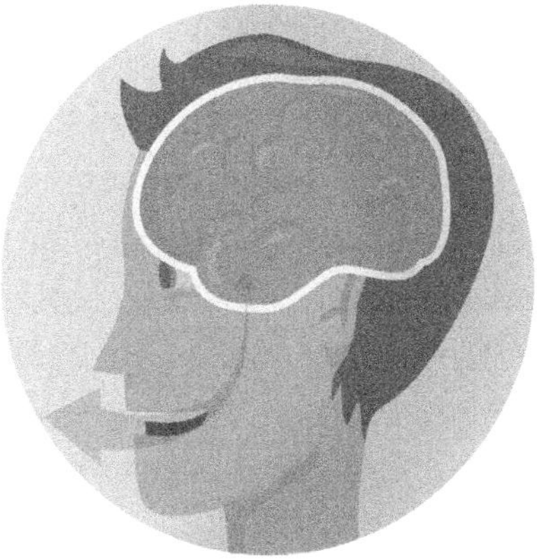

B.R.A.I.N is an easy way of remembering **the right questions to ask** so that you're fully informed on anything that's suggested or recommended to you at any point during pregnancy, labor, or birth. Conversations can sometimes crop up that can be overwhelming or unexpected. As a supportive birth partner, making sure that you're aware of B.R.A.I.N and able to help gather the right information by asking the right questions will allow you to both discuss what's being put forward and come to a decision. Which brings us to what it actually stands for:

Benefits – what are the benefits of accepting this choice presented to us? Are there any benefits in declining it?

Risks – are there any risks involved if you were to accept? Are there any risks in declining?

Alternatives – are there any alternatives we could consider and discuss?

Instincts – what are our instincts telling us? Trust your instincts, they're valid and important. Your partner has been growing your baby, feeling them move, and their instinct is key. But so is yours – you know your partner and this pregnancy too.

Nothing – can we simply do nothing and wait? If we were to do nothing, what would the benefits and risks be? Is inaction the right action here?

With each of these, you want to make sure you get both sides of the story for what's being suggested and discussed with you, and the potential impact it would have on your partner and the baby. In that vein, your partner and baby are individuals, unique – and what might be statistically or otherwise best for someone else may not be best for them. In your unique circumstance, understanding the facts and reasons why your partner is recommended X, Y, or Z is vital for her to make an informed decision.

As with anything in pregnancy, labor, or birth, informed consent is absolutely needed before anything can take place. That includes scans, blood tests, vaginal examinations, inductions, injections, and the list goes on. But before consent can be given, the other operative word is *informed*. Consent can only be informed if you have all of the relevant facts to make the decision. If you're given statistics, you can ask to see the research that supports them. If you're given general practice, ask why it became general practice. One perfect example of this is ice chips.

It's common practice in hospitals for women not to be allowed to eat during birth. Why? Well, there's a few reasons. The first stems from "Twilight Sleep" and similar early-anesthetic practices where women were numbed from the neck down and often choked on food or vomit. However, as modern anesthetic practices have changed to only numb women's bodies from the waist down, the "no food or drink" rule is still in place in many hospitals. Most recently, the defense you might hear for why women can't eat food or drink during labor is that a full stomach adds another hurdle in the event of a caesarean birth. But in 2007, the *American College of Obstetrics and Gynecology* actually changed their restrictions on eating and drinking during labor due to overwhelming evidence that it didn't pose a significant risk of asphyxiation during a caesarean birth.

That was 2007, so the reason the practice has remained isn't evidence-based, but tradition-based. Now, no eating may still be recommended in a high-risk pregnancy, but in a general low-risk pregnancy, food and water are fuel for the uterus, a muscle that is making its way through a marathon. In other words, if your partner is hungry, she should be able to eat. If she's thirsty, she should be able to drink.

So, DON'T PANIC, and use your B.R.A.I.N!

CREATING THE RIGHT ENVIRONMENT

We mentioned a little of this already in the anchors section, but the environment where birth happens can have an enormous impact on how your partner's body labors – even down to the ever-precarious balance of hormones. With that, it can stop, start, or even halt surges during labor altogether.

To imagine this a little better, let's start by looking at mammals in general. Let's say it's spring, on a farm, and lambs are beginning to be born. The farmer wants to be on hand if their sheep need any assistance, but they don't intervene otherwise. They are quiet, they don't disturb her, they stay back so she feels unobserved and safe.

If you have a pet cat and they're pregnant, you might make them a nice, cozy bed for when she comes to give birth. But, the majority of the time, they'll ignore that bed. They'll find somewhere that's dark, private, quiet, safe, and away from everyone else.

Are you starting to see the picture? All of these things that these mammals seek out and need for birth, are what we need too. We have basic needs of privacy, and need to feel safe and unobserved. Oxytocin loves this type of environment; one that's quiet, dark and peaceful. So, what can we do when it comes to creating the birth environment that's going to help facilitate the hormones that we need and help your partner to feel safe, calm, and comfortable? Well, there's a few things. First up:

Low Lighting - Think dimmed lights, candles, twinkling lights. Yeah, that's nice.

Having low lighting during labor helps your partner to feel relaxed. If you're planning a home birth, you have complete control over what's there and what you use – string up your Christmas lights or light candles around the room. If you're planning a hospital birth or going to a birthing center, you'll need to remember to take these items with you if your partner wants them there (note: no naked flames though! You can buy battery-powered candles which do just as good a job).

And remember you can dim the bright fluorescent lights in your labor room too – they don't need to be on just because you're in a hospital setting! Just keep in mind that many nurses might come in and turn the lights back up to do their assessments so it'll like be on you to reset the atmosphere.

Undisturbed - When your partner is in labor, breathing through her surges, focusing on her body and what she's feeling, being disturbed can take her out of that bubble instantly. Being disturbed can also halt the hormones needed for labor, and result in that uptick of adrenaline. There are, sometimes, reasons why she may need to be disturbed – maybe there is an important question that only she can answer. But – and this is a big *but* – she shouldn't be *unnecessarily* disturbed. As the birth partner, questions could be directed to you in the first instance, or conversations could take place outside the room. These are things to keep in mind that can be put in your birth plan to minimize disturbances to your partner.

Unobserved - You might be thinking "but she'll be giving birth, the midwife or doctor or nurse will be observing her?" Yes, someone will be keeping an eye on how things are moving along. But from a distance, subtly, and quietly – that's the key, and again pop that specific into your birth plan.

Most midwives will do this anyway, but not all caretakers are the same, and there's a big difference between *being* observed and *feeling* observed. If you feel observed, you're more likely to lose a sense of privacy, and that loss of privacy can make you feel less safe. Cue adrenaline! If you're waiting at traffic lights and can sense the person in the car next to you is looking over, and they aren't asking for any Grey Poupon, you start to feel uneasy and on edge, don't you?

That'll be your adrenaline kicking in, readying your fight or flight response. In an ideal situation, your partner shouldn't feel uneasy or on edge, and she certainly doesn't need her fight or flight system kicking in.

Scent, Sound, & Sight - These three can really make a room feel completely different. Think back to when we talked about anchors. What anchors does your partner want? What has she been using during pregnancy that needs to be there when she's in labor? Essential oils, diffusers, playlists, relaxation scripts, sounds of the ocean, photos of loved ones, positive affirmations written down; these are a few examples of what might make up her birth environment. They'll be familiar to her, and when they're there in labor and during birth her mind will recognize them all and relate them to those feelings of calm and comfort that her body experiences every time they are there.

No matter where your partner gives birth, you can make the environment what you both want. Even in theater, if she has a caesarean birth, there are things you can do to alter the environment. You may request that music be played, that voices are kept quiet, that the lights around the room are dimmed, or that your partner has a scent nearby that she can smell on a warm cloth. It is important that you are aware of what your partner wants for her birth environment, which is why good communication during pregnancy is essential, and writing your birth plan is too. This helps you to discuss things as a team and understand what it is she wants and what you'll need to do. It is also useful for your health care providers, helping them understand what you both want for your positive birth experience.

> "We did do our fair amount of practice on our own. Not so much the touchy touchy stuff but Emma did a lot of breathing practice herself and we would listen to quite a lot of Ocean sounds on Alexa in the evenings. Which funnily enough I do think Luna probably heard inside the belly because when we carried on playing it after she was born it was an unbelievable tool for getting her to sleep. Very strange!"
>
> - Joe S. Tonbridge, UK.

CONTINUITY OF CARE

This last section is less of a tool, and focuses more on your role as the birth partner and how you can use this toolset to craft and maintain the chair of positive birth.

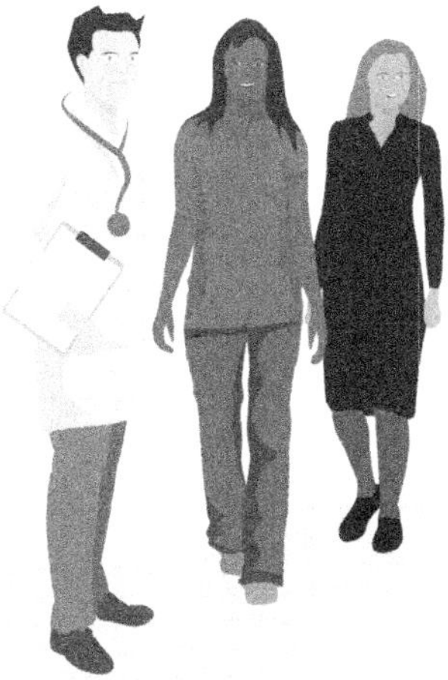

Unfortunately, it's quite common that you're unlikely to see the same doctors or midwives throughout pregnancy right through to birth. Resources, funding, the healthcare system being stretched pretty thin – all these contribute to the fact there is little to no continuity of care in birth. If you're planning a home birth, this isn't the case. With a home birth, chances are you'll have met the whole team at least a few times over and for that, you're very likely to know the midwife that attends the birth pretty well.

However, everywhere else, it's not that common. Continuity of care might not sound like a big deal on the surface, but it really can be. Forging familiar, trusting relationships form the basis of a positive birth experience. Your partner and you having those people around you at the birth that you trust, know, and feel safe with is important.

But who else, aside from midwives and doctors could that be? **You.**

As the birth partner, you will be by your partner's side from day one through to when she gives birth and beyond. You know her, her pregnancy, and your baby incredibly well. She feels safe with you, she trusts you, you're familiar, supportive, and reassuring. *You* are her absolute continuity of care. Because of that, never underestimate just how important it is that you are by your partner's side.

BRING THE WHOLE TOOLSET!

So, there you have it. A range of techniques and tools that you and your partner can use and call upon when your baby is ready to be born. But we want to end this section by going back to the beginning.

These tools are incredibly powerful and beneficial, but they are just a dip in the ocean of what hypnobirthing encompasses. Eliminating fears and anxieties around birth and replacing them with a positive, calm, and empowered mindset is at the heart of the entire practice, and this is achieved through a deep level of understanding and knowledge of labor and birth.

This means knowing what's going on in your partner's body when in labor, what her birth rights are, whether she feels in control of her birth and the choices being made, and whether you both know the options available to you. All of this will help your partner to have trust in her body and the baby. Feeling informed, alongside the tools and techniques that hypnobirthing covers, is what, we hope, will lead to a positive birth experience for your partner and yourself. No matter what that birth looks like, or where or how it happens, if your partner feels confident, informed, and part of the decision-making process, you're on the right path.

Now let's bring this all together!

"I enjoyed the visualisation exercises - the way it helped control your breathing and state of mind. I also found the anchor techniques really helped calm my partner down and she really valued that."

- Vijay J. Surrey, UK.

"With Hypnobirthing you can kind of just come into birth knowing that you're in like a safe protected space and it's just you and the Hypnobirthing exercises. However you're going to use them, it's your baby and that's all that kind of matters. That's how it's felt when I've been there and that the whole setting feels more relaxed and more calm. There's not more pressure or anything. It's just that. That's what we're here for. Let's keep calm safe. So that's what it felt."

- Mike B. Pwllheli, Wales

"The thing that surprised me most was how effective the techniques and mantras that Amanda used were in helping her to remain calm throughout the majority of the labour process. This included a long car journey to the hospital. Amanda also used the hypnobirthing techniques in a number of different settings (hospital (non-waterbirth), home (waterbirth) and in hospital again (waterbirth) with our 3 children's labours and it was just as effective in every setting. Also, the techniques she learnt during her hypnobirthing sessions have been useful in other aspects of life as well for relaxation/meditation/mindfulness."

- Phil L. North Oxfordshire, UK

CHAPTER FOUR

BEFORE THE BIRTH

WHAT YOU'RE GOING TO LEARN:

- The first steps of using hypnobirthing in practice to get ready for birth
- The big decisions to make with your partner before the birth
- Context for the options of where and how you can choose to give birth
- A roster for who can make up your birthing team
- The questions to ask and how to craft your very own birth plan

This is where the rhythm of the race changes. Up until now we've talked to you a lot about the philosophy, history, and science of hypnobirthing – but now we're going to put all that we've learned and more into practice. In doing so, we're also going to finally put an end to the dreaded pair of birth partner questions:

"What can I do? How can I help?"

When your partner is in labor, those questions might constantly be circling your head as a birth partner. Unfortunately, if your partner is in labor, there might be no worse time to ask them out loud. As you might expect, she's a little busy at the moment.

By that point, she's already deep in the trenches. She's trying her best to block out distractions as she focuses in on herself, her breathing, and her body. She's working to embrace her role in all of this while she experiences a number of emotions, changes, challenges, and sensations she may have never felt before. All while you can't help but wonder: *am I one of those distractions?*

Your heart is in the right place by asking those questions; it's just that your timing could use some work. You obviously want to support her throughout the experience – but not knowing what support you can offer, or how you can actually help, likely won't do much more than distract her from what she's focused on doing – birthing your baby. Because of that, we can almost guarantee that she either won't be able to give, or simply won't have, the answers you're looking for.

And if you don't have those answers by the time you're in that room, you might find yourself in a place where many dads have been before – standing on the sidelines. Huddled in the corner of that room feeling useless, anxious, and worried as we wait for something miraculous to happen. We become the spectators, fans in stadium seats sometimes too nervous to even cheer for our partners, unsure if that's something they'd want, on one of the most important days of both of our lives.

Although knowing what to do and how to help are both important questions to have answered, those answers have to be found, studied, and practiced long before labor even begins. You're still *before the birth* right now, but a lot of moments during pregnancy and close to the birth can have us feeling like we're being dropped in the deep end with no life preserver. In those moments, it really is sink or swim. But just like all the things that seemed to have gotten glossed over when growing up – how to write a check, pay taxes, properly boil noodles, trim nose hair – has anyone actually taught us? Has anyone shown us or explained in detail why it's important to be a good birth partner?

A positive birth experience only happens when our partners feel **confident, safe, in control, and empowered**. And a positive birth experience, just like a negative one, can cascade too. So, before the birth, let's nail down our answers to a few of the most looming questions that lead up to the big event: *where, how, and who?*

Where do you want to give birth? **How** do you want to give birth? And **who** do you want in that room with you? The only way to make these decisions, however, is to understand them, along with some of the benefits and drawbacks of each.

To begin, let's start with the *where:*

WHERE?

There are three main options for where you and your partner can give birth: a hospital, a birthing center, or at home. We've had dads experience birth at each of them and each choice has its share of benefits and drawbacks. The best way to decide which is right for you is to determine what a positive birth looks like to you. To help you in that regard, we're going to outline a defense for each choice. Firstly...

IN DEFENSE OF HOSPITAL BIRTH

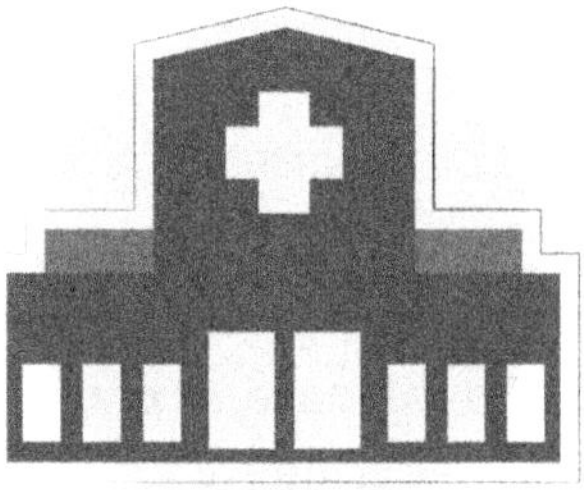

Representing nearly 84% of all births, hospital births are by far the most commonplace to have a baby. When taking into account conventional wisdom about births, this makes sense. Even if we don't agree, birth is still often seen as a medical procedure rather than a natural process – and hospitals are where most of us feel medical procedures are *supposed* to happen. To add to that, hospitals fall under general health insurance coverage and the big question of "what if complications arise during labor?" has a clear answer at the hospital – after all, where else would you go for a medical emergency?

We're not saying that hospitals are dangerous or bad for birth, only that in some cases they can't change as fast as culture can. As practices like hypnobirthing and evidence-based birth continue to gain more ground, there is likely to be a shift in how hospital births are done. That doesn't mean hospitals suddenly won't become the primary place people give birth, but many of them will likely adapt their regulations to adhere to new studies and best practices – something that's already happening in many hospitals across the U.S, U.K, and many parts of the rest of the world.

In fact, many of our dads that had recent hospital births consider them to be positive birth experiences. While most acknowledged that was only because they went into the whole process well-prepared, it's still a good sign for things to come. The key to finding the right hospital for you, one that listens to your personal beliefs and desires for the birth, is simply doing your research. The closest hospital to you may not be the right one, and you're never locked in to your first choice if you don't feel comfortable. Reach out, try different options and find the right fit – there's usually quite a few to choose from.

HOSPITAL BIRTH STORY

"We had a hospital birth. Claire was induced because we were 13 days beyond our due date. She had a pessary induction, so they were expecting progress to be steady, but Claire's pessary sort of put her at 100 miles an hour straightaway. So we basically had all this stuff planned from the hypnobirthing course for the early phase, where we were going to watch a movie, Claire was going to have a bath, we were going to go for a walk in the woods, and have a glass of wine. All these things that we had planned for that initial phase, because we were expecting it to be gradual and slow and nice. We were going to make the oxytocin go right through the roof! But unfortunately the initial phase went out the window a bit because Claire came in straight away and she was going through quite intense surgeries from the off. Although she was in a fair amount of pain. I know that the Hypnobirthing helped her embrace that pain and not feel scared by it. Then when we got into the hospital it was a million miles an hour. So we went in at 10 o'clock, and she started pushing at 11 - so it was really fast!"

- Adam R. Brighton, UK.

IN DEFENSE OF HOME BIRTH

Only a little over 2% of all births take place at home, making it the most uncommon place to have a baby. In recent years, especially as a result of the COVID-19 pandemic, that number has steadily climbed as home births are often seen as a safe, relaxing way for low-risk pregnancies to experience a natural birth.

Typically led by a certified professional midwife, naturopathic midwife, or licensed nurse-midwife, rather than a doctor, home births are almost always vaginal births with minimal medication. They often implement a variety of mind-body techniques like hypnobirthing and emphasize preparation to reduce any pain from childbirth, limit any adrenaline production, and promote a safe birthing environment.

Taking place at home in a room of your choice, home births are also often accompanied by doulas and very commonly revolve around water births for at least some portion of the labor process. The biggest drawbacks of home births come in the form of risks associated with pregnancy. In the event of a medical emergency, midwives do have the tools to handle emergencies, but they don't have as many at their disposal as a hospital would. Because of that, the dreaded "what if complications arise during labor?" turns many women away from the idea. In general, low-risk home births have the **highest percentage of success rates** and the **lowest percentage of interventions**. It should be noted of course, that the data collection for this is impacted by the fact that there are fewer home births than hospital births.

In regards to the fear of the "what if something goes wrong?" question, you should know that midwives are very frequently averse to taking risks – if complications arise that could be dangerous, they'll likely be the first to recommend a transfer to the hospital. That being said, almost 45% of first-time mothers who choose a home birth find themselves transferring to hospitals from the general fear of "what if", and yet only 12% of second-time mothers' transfer. You always feel more confident the second time around – and you can also feel more confident with the decision for a home birth if your first experience was traumatic elsewhere.

One takeaway from that is that maybe a home birth may not be the choice you and your partner are comfortable with for your first baby, but you might have more confidence and feel more in control for your second. At that point, like many other parents, you know far better what to expect. Even so, as we mentioned in the hospital section, the other takeaway is that **preparation is key.**

We encourage you to do your own research – to meet with a home birth midwife and their team and see if it's something you'd like to explore. There are massive benefits to home birth:

- you're in your own environment
- you feel safe
- there is immediate privacy and familiarity
- you're surrounded by familiar smells, sights, and comforts of home
- you're less likely to have epidurals or an instrumental birth

- you're less likely to have an episiotomy or tearing
- and after the birth, you're already home with your baby!

All of these various benefits are conducive to what we talk about the most in hypnobirthing: creating a positive birth experience. They all help to encourage oxytocin production, create a sense of calmness, and help you and your partner feel in control, all whilst discouraging adrenaline, fear, and the possibility of birth trauma. Because of all these benefits, most all hypnobirthing experts lean in favor of home births – acknowledging most of all that you and your partner know how to do this, and you *can* do this.

One final benefit of home birth is that it's the only option that comes with continuity of care inherent in the package. The team you meet at the beginning is the same you will get to know throughout the process. When it's time for the birth, that same team will be there to guide you and your partner through all of it. Hospitals and most birthing centers can't guarantee that sort of continuity of care.

HOME BIRTH STORY

"We wanted to do it on our own together at home, and we knew there were medical professionals in a building just down the road, just in case. It was terrifying, scary, nerve wracking, joyous, wonderful, miraculous. For eight hours we were going through various stages, but neither of us panicked because we both knew what was coming. We both knew our roles. Through Hypnobirthing I felt I had a purpose at birth. I was able to be involved with the breathing techniques and the positive affirmations - which gave us both some common ground. Birth can be scary but we had a plan, and a backup plan, and as we'd been practicing we felt really comfortable. So we started off with massage techniques and when the pain got stronger, we'd move to the tens machine, and then the next step would be entering the pool. I felt prepared enough to support her. And she trusted me both in terms of learning the same plan, as well the same techniques. The hospital said if we have to go to the hospital that's fine. But we made a decision to stay at home. We didn't want to let go of that home birth anyway, so I actually got the chance to deliver Millie myself which was a wonderful moment."

- Adam W. Royal Leamington Spa, UK.

IN DEFENSE OF A BIRTHING CENTER

Rounding out the remaining 14% of all births, a birthing center is often seen as somewhat of a middle ground or the best of both worlds between hospital and home. Depending on the birthing center you find, the setting can often be relaxing and far more home-like than a hospital. While obviously not as homey as your home, they still offer a number of mind and body support options to make your partner as comfortable as possible during labor and birth.

Additionally, birthing centers often have easy access to tubs for water births and have doulas readily available for guidance and support should you need them. Often the goal of birthing centers is simply allowing the mother to have the birth experience they want. To do that, many have access to almost everything a hospital would, including Pitocin, to encourage labor and medications for pain management.

However, take that with a grain of salt as some birthing centers across the U.S. are limited by laws and hospital policy, meaning they're only approved for tools to assist such as oxygen and a limited supply of Pitocin used only in case of emergency. They may also not have access to anesthesiologists to administer an epidural and emergency equipment in the event that something like a caesarean birth is necessary. In that event, just like a home birth, transfer to a hospital would be necessary.

Often, birthing centers are strategically built to adjoin hospitals or be very close by – so that transfer is very likely to be a quick one.

With all that in mind, let's look at *how* you can choose to give birth.

BIRTHING CENTER STORY

"I remember her surges started around dinner time (7pm at her parents). By midnight they were getting pretty regular and we knew we should start thinking about heading to the birthing center (1hr car ride away).

I think we got to the BC at about 2am and settled in. It was a large room with a large low bed that she could get in and out of easily and a large tub. They also had different birthing balls (large ones and peanut ones), as well as some other hanging ropes that she could bear down on.

Our daughter was not actually born until 4pm, so there were moments of transitioning from the bed to the tub and back. I was able to talk and keep her mind on her safe place and repeat affirmations that we had for the birth.

Towards the end she was transferred to the surgical room next door because our daughter was stuck coming out. This move was pretty fast and confusing for me because french is definitely not my first language (still learning) and medical french is way out of my league. So in those moments I used some calming and safe place techniques to center myself before someone could explain to me what exactly was going on in broken English while handing me a pair of scrubs. Soon after that I was able to get back to my wife and they were able to guide our daughter out without too much intervention. "

- Aaron K. New York, US.

HOW?

There are ultimately two ways to birth a baby – **a vaginal birth** or **a caesarean birth**. Within those two ways there is a lot of variety and wiggle room, but at the foundation of it, a baby is either birthed through the birth canal and out the vagina, or they are surgically removed from the uterus during a caesarean birth. To start off:

IS A VAGINAL BIRTH PART OF YOUR POSITIVE BIRTH PLAN?

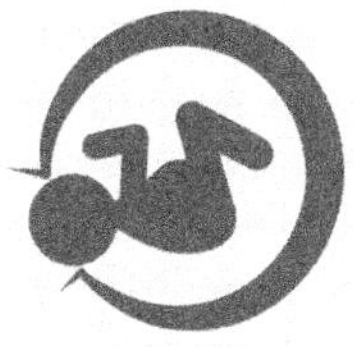

Making up about 70% of all births, a vaginal birth is exactly as the name entails; the baby is birthed through the vagina after exiting the uterus and making their way down through the birth canal. However, a vaginal birth is dependent on a number of factors – one of which being that predicting when labor begins is very hard to do.

All women and all babies are different but the average time to give birth occurs after carrying a baby to *term* – which means around 38-42 weeks of pregnancy. Within that timeline is early and late term, but all of those hold the implication that everything is ready on the baby's end to be born. The reason we mention that is because (barring induction) a vaginal birth usually happens on the timeline of the baby.

A caesarean birth, on the other hand, can technically occur anytime post-term, though the trend of elective caesarean births without a medical reason is something many health professionals warn against. Instead, they recommend that women have, or at least plan to have a vaginal birth unless there is a pressing medical reason to get a caesarean birth.

NATURAL VS. MEDICATED

We mentioned there's quite a bit of wiggle room when it comes to vaginal birth and that's definitely true. The most common difference you might hear about is between a natural or a medicated vaginal birth.

A natural birth is exactly as it sounds, a birth how it might occur in nature - or as it might have occurred in the cave with you standing guard all those thousands of years ago. A natural birth often refers to a birth with no medication or medical intervention. As you might expect, the other side of that is a vaginal birth that does have medication or medical interventions.

That being said, it's best to look at those two options as the extremes. Within those extremes is where the majority of vaginal births fall. They might be women who don't want an epidural or coached pushing, but they might be perfectly fine with an IV and even some Pitocin. There might also be women who receive an epidural but still want to experience all they can during the process from watching the baby be born to holding them for the "Golden Hour" afterward.

If your partner's goal is a natural birth, there are likely decisions they are firm on but there also might be others where some flexibility is okay. Conversely, just because your partner wants a medicated birth doesn't mean they are accepting of every single type of medical intervention available. Having those conversations to find you and your partner's ideal center is extremely important for both of you, and it's something we'll get into more very soon. But first, we want to bring your attention to something hypnobirthing experts are extremely fond of:

THE BEAUTY OF WATER BIRTHS

A type of birth where your partner is immersed in water at some point during the birth process (whether labor or the actual birth), water birth was first reported by a medical journal in 1805. However, for anyone that has seen *Apocalypto*, there was nothing stopping us from water births far earlier. In fact, South Pacific Islanders were known to give birth in shallow waters and pharoahs of Egypt were intentionally birthed in water. Actually, ancient Egypt has a lot of interesting birthing techniques and documented history worth looking at. Also, they've been praising moms for 8,000 years!

"Repay your mother for all her care. Give her as much bread as she needs, and carry her as she carried you, for you were a heavy burden to her. When you were finally born, she still carried you on her neck and for three years she suckled you and kept you clean."

But back to water birth. Water birth didn't regain popularity until the late 1980s and early 90s. It is especially popular for home births but has actually made its way into quite a few hospitals and birthing centers. The basic premise is that you set up a tub, control the temperature, and your partner is free to splash around during surges of labor and even stay in for the birth of the baby.

The value of water birth actually comes from massive benefits to both mother and baby. For the mother, water births can help to:

- Reduce the intensity of surges which can reduce the need for medication
- Speed up the labor process
- Allow for tons of movement and various labor positions
- Encourage calm and control - that warm water is heavenly!
- Can reduce the likelihood of perineal tears/trauma if used for birth
- Can reduce access from care providers, offering a more undisturbed birth

For babies born through water births, it can help to:

- Ease the transition to the world as they go from amniotic fluid to water
- Allow for immediate skin-to-skin contact with the mother, encouraging a number of natural hormones to help them get their bearings.

The other beauty of water birth is that sometimes you're invited! In many stories from our dads that have done water birth, they've put on their swimsuits and sat behind their partners, holding them as they bear down through surges and helping them feel safe and calm. Even without getting in the tub, you have your partner in close vicinity to hold your hand if needed, to rest and talk to you as they move into different positions for labor and even birth.

With all that said, we know water births aren't for everyone, but even using it to ease the intense surges of labor and increase that oxytocin production might be something worth talking about with your partner and providers.

IS A CAESAREAN BIRTH PART OF YOUR POSITIVE BIRTH PLAN?

Rounding out the other 30% of all births, a caesarean birth is a major surgery where an incision is cut horizontally through the muscles of the abdomen and uterus in order to extract the baby without it having to be birthed through the vagina. A typical hospital stay after a caesarean birth is around 3-4 days to make sure the incision is healing properly. After that, full recovery can take around eight weeks.

In the past 40 or so years, the rate of caesarean birth births has skyrocketed from 1 of every 20 births, to around 1 of every 3 – so really, 30-33%. Interestingly, the World Health Organization (WHO) says that the recommended rate for caesarean births should only be about 10-15% to improve outcomes. Higher levels than that are showing that caesarean births aren't being used only in the case of medical emergencies, but rather as an elective operation.

A caesarean birth, to many women, is an option perceived as "pain-free" or to give control. A major reason for women electing for the operation is to have some control over the unpredictability in labor and birth. In that way, caesearean births fit in line with a birthing culture that is increasingly risk-averse, with a lack of systems designed to support physiology. As they are numbed from just above the waist down, and often not put entirely under anesthesia, women are unable to feel anything during the birth but are still able to see the baby being born.

Because of that and a multitude of other personal reasons, caesarean births have become sought after by many women even without a medical reason for it, and many hospitals welcome their wishes of an elective caesarean birth. While there is nothing at all inherently wrong with this, as we mentioned *anything* can be a positive birth experience, a lot of women aren't always made aware of the risks associated with caesarean births before receiving them.

Something that often gets glazed over is that caesarean births are a *major* surgery, and like any major surgery, they have the possibility of complications. In the case of caesarean births, those complications could be an infection of the uterus, surgical injury to the bladder or intestines, amniotic fluid embolism (where amniotic fluid or other fetal fluid enters the mother's blood), possible infant laceration from the scalpel, hemorrhaging, and an increased risk for any future pregnancies or the possibility of future vaginal delivery.

The other thing to be aware of with caesarean births is in the case of Emergency caesarean births. While we absolutely don't think that most hospitals resort to caesarean births unless it actually is a medical emergency, we also know how common that occurrence can be. Whether caesarean births are decided upon as a result of the mother "failing to progress" or otherwise, it's a good idea to look at caesarean birth rates at any hospital you choose and the rates of your attending doctor.

In that way, the place you choose to give birth has a massive impact. If the rates of the hospital you want to go, or the doctor presiding over you, have higher caesarean birth rates than the WHO recommended 10-15%, or more than the 30% average (we've seen hospitals with rates as high as 60%) you should make sure that a caesarean birth isn't something you and your birth partner fundamentally don't want. In these birth locations, interventions can start to cascade leading to an eventual caesearean birth– regardless of whether it was a part of your plan.

ARE THERE OTHER OPTIONS?

Now you have the two primary paths to birth, but as we mentioned, there's still quite a bit of nuance. We aren't going to go into detail about all the different methods of childbirth, but we do want to bring your attention to how these decisions can all be helped through hypnobirthing.

Above, we mentioned a lot about cacsarean births to the point where it might seem like hypnobirthing practices would be left at the door. It's a major surgery, right?

It definitely is, but there are different types of caesarean births. One kind that has gained a lot of popularity recently is called the "gentle caesarean" or "gentle caesarean birth". Gentle caesarean births are where the baby is gently being born from the abdomen. In some cases, care providers 'massage' the abdomen to almost mimic surges and the feeling of the baby making their way out gently. At the end, the care provider can then help the baby gently to the mother's chest. This type of caesarean birth isn't always possible if there is a medical need or emergency requiring the baby to be born via caesarean birth, but it's still a great opportunity to maintain control of the situation in a different birthing experience. Even delayed cord clamping can be offered in the case of caesarean births – some hospitals offer this routinely if the baby is born in good conditions.

In a gentle caesarean birth, you can still be there. You can still request low lighting for your partner (so long as it's safe in the theater), music can still be playing, voices can be kept low and soft, scripts can be read, curtains can be lowered so that the mother can see the delivery, and you can ask for delayed cord clamping during a "Golden Hour."

With those options laid out, it's also important to "go for a test drive" in a manner of speaking. The *where* of birth determines a lot of the other choices in birth. In that regard, we encourage multiple visits either to the hospital or the birthing center, or to the care providers that might preside over you to build a connection and mutual understanding. Through these conversations and visits, you'll also be better able to understand what's possible during the birth in comparison to your desires, and what isn't. For example, a midwife at home very likely won't be performing an elective caesarean birth, and a doctor in a hospital very likely won't be encouraging a water birth - especially if they don't have access to tubs in birthing rooms. Some hospitals do!

And finally, let's talk about *who* you want in the room with you.

WHO?

Just like raising a baby takes a village, often, so does birthing one. While it's true that some people have been known to perform successful free births, which is basically just them at home with no guidance or limited support – having the expertise of a select few individuals to rely on and help you through this whirlwind adventure can be extremely beneficial and make the birth experience safer overall.

Depending on where you choose to give birth, some of your options for who is in the room will be determined ahead of time. After all, doctors aren't really performing house calls anymore. Still, in that regard, it's good to know who is presiding over you no matter where you are. That way, whether you experience continuity of care or not, you still know the qualifications that got your providers to where they are in the first place.

To begin, let's start with:

DOCTORS

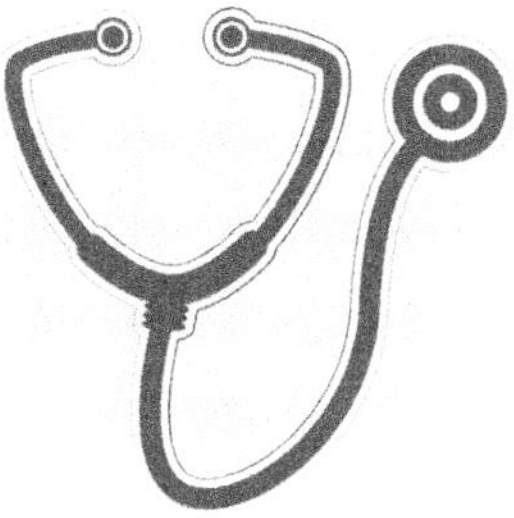

"Doctors" is a catch-all term, but the ones associated with birth are often OB-GYNs, or obstetrician-gynecologists. An OB-GYN is a doctor who has completed medical school and their residency (and often more) to garner expertise in female reproductive health, pregnancy, childbirth, and more. Unlike many primary care doctors, an OB-GYN is a medicinal and a surgical doctor. That means they can diagnose and prescribe medicine, and they are also trained to deal with birthing emergencies such as emergency caesarean births.

While OB-GYNs are extremely qualified and only receive their board certifications after rigorous testing, their schooling still often treats pregnancy as a medical emergency. With that, their expertise is colored by the experience of pregnancy in high-risk scenarios – ones where constant monitoring is needed, Pitocin is required to encourage contractions, painkillers and epidurals are commonplace, and natural, unobserved births are seen as riskier and more dangerous. Many OB-GYNs you meet will have less experience with an unmedicated, unmonitored, or natural birth.

In that way, doctors are often predisposed, through their education, to see pregnancy and birth in one highly-regulated way, and any alternative as dangerous. There's no question that a doctor in a hospital during an emergency situation offers the best chance of resolving that emergency – but that's the key thing to keep in mind – not all pregnancies are emergencies. Not all are high-risk or in need of constant interventions. However, if you ask an average doctor whether you should get a home birth, they'll often be adamantly against it.

When getting to know your doctors, it's essential to ask any questions that you and your partner have discussed to reduce the likelihood of any friction later on. However, keep in mind that doctors are on call - and the one you and your partner get to know and like, might not be working on the day of your baby's birth.

MIDWIVES

Midwives, similar to doctors, receive extensive medical training in women's health, but are most commonly known for birth and postpartum care. Generally, there are three levels of midwifery credentials: Certified Professional Midwife (CPM), Certified Midwife (CM), and Certified Nurse-Midwife (CNM).

Midwives often work alongside doctors in hospitals or alongside a team in birthing centers. In the event of an emergency, most are trained to handle complications that arise during pregnancy, but they have not received medical training to perform caesarean births.

Unlike doctors, midwives have often been known to incorporate a number of different practices in their repertories such as performing home births, water births, and freestanding births. Because they are trained to view and support birth as a natural process. As experts in physiology, they are able to recognize when there is a deviation from the norm and will offer intervention and refer to medical care only if clinically indicated. In that way, something like a caesarean birth would be a last resort.

When deciding on a midwife, it's important to be aware of the relationship they're building with your partner. Ask your partner questions to see if they trust this particular care provider and if they can imagine the sort of comfort they'd feel with them presiding over them on the big day.

DOULAS

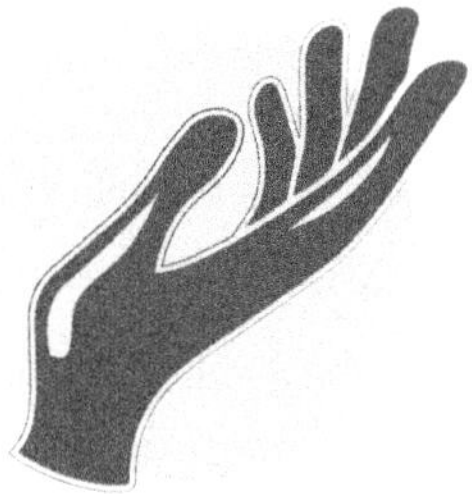

Doulas are birth practitioners that are quickly becoming more popular every year. They typically don't have formal obstetric training or go through the extensive education of midwives, but their responsibility is the most similar to yours when it comes to birth. They are there to make sure the mother's voice is heard and that they feel calm and relaxed. With a number of practices and homey touches that we've outlined already, designed to make the birthing environment feel warm and welcoming, they allow mothers to focus all of their attention on birth.

Without you taking on the role of birth partner, many expectant mothers hire doulas to do precisely what you're practicing. While the midwife and the doctor may be more focused on the baby and the birth, you and the doula are focused on the mother and the experience of birth – and making it as positive as possible.

That being said, having a doula in addition to your being there is only a benefit for the entire process. Sometimes the excessive focus on being your partner's advocate, making them feel safe, or being on constant high alert with everything going on, can have you unable to enjoy the experience too. Sharing that responsibility with an experienced doula can take a little of that pressure off your shoulders. In planning ahead, you can also have post-natal doulas who help out post-birth – doing anything from making food for the family to holding the baby while you and your partner rest.

LABOR NURSES

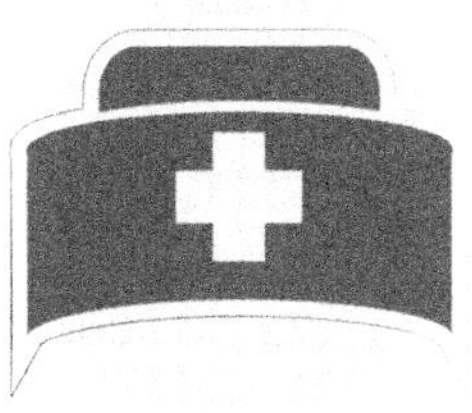

When giving birth in a hospital, labor nurses are often the unsung heroes of the entire endeavor. Although the decisions for care are approved by the doctor or OB-GYN presiding, the labor nurses are the ones you are likely to see the most throughout your entire hospital stay.

They are the ones who are checking in on fetal monitoring, answering calls for any concerns, and being there to support mothers through labor and birth. They are also the ones who you're more likely to get to know throughout the experience. As we mentioned, if you plan to give birth anywhere other than at home, the continuity of care you experience is often nonexistent. In that way, labor nurses play a large part in the experience for many expectant mothers.

That being said, a hospital is a 24-hour business and everyone has shifts. If you stay the night or throughout a full day, the labor nurses on staff will change just like the doctors. The first nurses you and your partner might have absolutely adored, but the next you might not have gotten along as well with.

These things have been known to happen in hospitals and birthing centers. Forrest Gump would say it's "like a box of chocolates, you never know what you're going to get." The OB-GYN that you visited the most during the pregnancy might not be on shift when your partner goes into labor. If she was relying on the trust she built with that particular doctor, that turn of events might throw her off.

The same can happen with midwives. Because of that, your role is even more vital. You are the consistency. You are the continuity. You are an anchor for her. Even if the doctor, midwife, and nurses change multiple times over the course of the labor and on to the birth, *you* are going to be there through it all.

BIRTH PLANS & STOPLIGHTS

At this point, you have a better understanding of some of the decisions you're going to be faced with when it comes to labor and birth. You've read a little history, you've seen a little science, you've heard about the where, the how, and the who, and you've gathered a few of the tools that will help lead to a positive birth experience.

Now, it's time to put it all together.

The birth plan is a written document that you design yourself and fill in with your partner. Ultimately, it becomes a physical document that you can make copies of and send to your doctor, midwife, or doula and even pin on the wall of whatever room you choose to give birth in. But more than that, it's an opportunity to present you and your partner with every option available for the birth and then open up communication and dialogue to decide which ones will best contribute to a positive birth experience.

The best thing we've found to keep in mind when crafting a birth plan is the **Stoplight Method**. The stoplight method is as simple as it sounds: *red* means **stop,** *green* means **go,** and *yellow* means **slow down.**

In the context of your birth plan, red are the things you and your partner absolutely do not want in your birth. Red is where you stop and stand your ground. Green, on the other hand, means the things you absolutely do want to have in your birth. Green is everything that's good to go. And finally, yellow are the things that you feel okay going either way on. Maybe you'll push through the light, or maybe you'll come to a full stop. Yellow is perfect for preferences that you would want only in the case of emergencies.

Having this mentality of the stoplight when creating your birth plan can also open the door for communication with your partner during the actual birth. It can even be the stepping-stone to your own unique form of dialogue and observation when in labor.

If your partner is sure that something isn't right during the birth, "Red." If she's worried something might be wrong, "Yellow." If everything seems good, and she seems to be calm, in control – things are "Green." Hand signals, a quick safeword even – anything can be decided on previously to stop something when she suddenly feels unsure, scared, or out of control.

To add to all of that, a birth plan doesn't have to be the "definitive edition" the first time you both talk about it. Before the birth, it's meant to open the door to honest communication about some exciting and some difficult decisions. With that in mind, we like to break it down into **five categories** where you try to answer as many questions as you can. Below, we're going to list the categories and the questions you'd like answers to.

THE BASICS

- Where would you like to give birth?
  - ☐ Hospital ______________________________
  - ☐ Home ______________________________
  - ☐ Birthing center ______________________________
- Who would you like on the birthing team?
  - ☐ Midwife ______________________________
  - ☐ Doula ______________________________
  - ☐ Doctor/labor nurse ______________________________
  - ☐ You! ______________________________
- Would you be okay with medical students or student midwives observing or helping? Many teaching hospitals and midwifery encourage births to be observed by aspiring care providers to give them hands-on experience. You can say "no" to this request, but it's also important that they ask anyway, so that you know ahead of time the qualifications of the staff presiding. Yes ☐ No ☐ ______________________________
- How would you like to give birth?
  - ☐ Vaginal ______________________________
  - ☐ Natural/unmedicated ______________________________
  - ☐ Caesarean birth ______________________________
  - ☐ Gentle caesarean birth ______________________________
  - ☐ Water birth ______________________________
- Are any other people, like family and friends, allowed in the room during birth?
  - ☐ Are visitors welcome immediately after or when would be ideal? ______________________________
  - ☐ Would you like the birth recorded, photographed, or no pictures to be taken at all? ______________________________

PAIN MANAGEMENT

- What kind of pain management techniques might be right for you?
  - ☐ (These can be medications or practices like those found in hypnobirthing!) Yes ☐ No ☐ ______________________
    ____
- Would your partner want to move into different positions during labor? Yes ☐ No ☐ ______________________
- Would they like to have a tub available for labor? Yes ☐ No ☐ ______________________________
- Would your partner want to get an epidural?
  - Epidurals have become one of the main pain-management systems used for birth. It is an anesthetic injected into the space around the spinal cord to numb a woman's body from the waist down.
  - Typically, your partner can receive an epidural when they are in active labor (4-5 cm dilated). It is too late to place an epidural when your partner is fully dilated (10 cm).
  - Epidurals not only help with pain management, but can also be used to help speed along the labor process for someone who has labored for a long time. Yes ☐ No ☐
- Some things to keep in mind with epidurals:
- There are two types:
  - A regular epidural injects directly to the lower spine and is hooked to a small catheter in that area to drip or pump the medicine. A combined spinal epidural (CSE) is where a local anesthetic is given to the lower spine, and then a needle tap is done and attached to the drip or pump. Yes ☐ No ☐

PAIN MANAGEMENT

- They can lower blood pressure, give severe headaches, often prolong labor, cause urinary infrequency and necessitate a urinary catheter, have been known to increase the use of forceps or vacuums for birth, increase the likelihood of severe tears, and in rare cases, have been known to cause infection.
- Post-partum, epidurals have also been known to cause severe back-pain at the injection site in many mothers and often severe headaches as well. Yes ☐ No ☐
- Would your partner want to get an IV?
  - (An IV, or intravenous drip feed, is standard practice for many hospitals in caring for pregnant patients. It not only ensures that the patient stays hydrated, but also provides the doctors or nurses with a direct line to administer medications. Pain management, Pitocin, all can be administered through the IV. To that end, it's important to know that if your partner wants an unmedicated birth, an IV is something you are allowed to say "no" to, but there may be pushback. If there is no immediate medical reason for an IV in a hospital, it will often be used only for hydration as they may not allow food or fluid by mouth.) Yes ☐ No ☐
- A good compromise you can help your partner and provider come to on this is a hep-lock or saline lock, where the needle is inserted and taped down just in case, but no IV line is actually attached
  - Some things to keep in mind with IVs are that they: Restrict the movement of the pregnant woman, making it harder to get into differing laboring positions.

PAIN MANAGEMENT

    - Can over-hydrate the pregnant patient causing increased swelling in hands, feet, and breasts.
- Can artificially inflate the baby's weight at birth, resulting in weight loss 3-5 days post-birth >7%.
- **Important Note:** Babies will always lose some weight in the days after birth, but numbers close to or at 10% can cause providers to express concern over the weight and many mothers (if they are breastfeeding) to worry that they are not producing enough milk, increasing the likelihood of supplementing with formula.

COMFORT & ENVIRONMENT

- Do you want music playing in the room? Yes ☐ No ☐ ________
- Does your partner want to wear their own clothes or a birthing gown? Yes ☐ No ☐ ____________________________
- Do you want any essential oils for smells? Yes ☐ No ☐ ______
- Do you want lights strung up? Yes ☐ No ☐ _______________
- Would you like an affirmation poster hung up? Yes ☐ No ☐
- Are there any dietary restrictions? Yes ☐ No ☐ ____________
- Do you want to catch the baby? Yes ☐ No ☐ _______________

THE UNEXPECTED

- If labor isn't progressing, are there any interventions you would approve?

THE UNEXPECTED

- ☐ Membrane stripping: This is a method for inducing labor where a care provider will sweep their gloved finger between the thin membranes of the amniotic sac to separate it.
- ☐ Foley bulb: This is a procedure where a doctor inserts a catheter into the cervix. Once in place, they inflate it like a balloon with saline water, putting pressure on the cervix to encourage dilation.
- ☐ Breaking of the waters: This is the artificial rupture of the membranes (AROM). The membranes often rupture naturally, but if they do not, a care provider might do it as a means of encouraging labor. However, breaking of the waters, or the amniotic sac, puts a timer on the birth for most providers as the insulation protecting the baby is now gone.
- ☐ Pitocin: This is synthetic oxytocin that's meant to encourage contractions and speed up the labor process. We know we've talked about it already but it's one of the most common interventions to induce and progress labor.
- ☐ Prostaglandins: These are lipid compounds that can be given orally or vaginally, and they serve to soften an otherwise hard and closed cervix. They are often used first (sometimes with a foley bulb), and AROM or Pitocin is used afterward to continue the induction process. One in particular, Cytotec, is used in the U.S. and has been discovered to have some severe side effects - namely it can cause labor to proceed a little too quickly and cause the baby distress.

THE UNEXPECTED

- If the baby is breech (going to be born feet-first rather than head-first) what would you like to do? Nothing, attempt to rotate, or potentially a caesarean birth? ☐
- If the baby appears stuck in the birth canal, do you approve of the use of forceps or a vacuum? ☐
- Where do you stand on caesarean births? Would you want one only as a last resort in an emergency situation after every other option has been exhausted? ☐
- If the baby or mother's life is at risk, what's the plan? ☐
- If the baby has to go to the NICU (neonatal intensive care unit) would you want to go there immediately with them? ☐

POSTPARTUM

- Would you like to cut the umbilical cord? ☐
- Do you want to keep the placenta? ☐
- Do you want to save any of the cord blood? ☐
- Do you want lo be able to hold the baby immediately for skin-to-skin contact and experience the "Golden Hour?" ☐
- Do you want to be with the baby for any procedures or measurements? ☐
- Do you want to delay any procedures or measurements? ☐
- Does your partner want to breastfeed immediately? ☐
- Do you want to delay the first bath and receive any help when it occurs? ☐
- If it's a boy, do you want them to be circumcised? ☐

No matter where you decide to give birth or who you decide to be involved, creating a birth plan as early as possible is extremely helpful. That way, when you get to know your midwife, or tour your hospital, you'll be able to talk about the plan early enough to get a reading on what your caregivers would approve or not. It isn't guaranteed that every doctor or midwife you encounter will be 100% on board with your birth plan, which is why it's important to communicate with them as much as you can ahead of time. In addition to that, it's important to keep your stoplights in mind.

Where can we not bend on our decisions? *What are the red lights?*

Where can we offer a little leeway? *What are the yellow lights?*

What are we looking for in our positive birth experience? *What are the green lights?*

Communicating, writing things down, completing your birth plan, and then talking about it with your chosen healthcare provider is the true foundation of a positive birth experience. Because when you get to the third trimester, and into the last weeks before the expected birth date, it might already be too late.

In those last weeks, it's hard to predict when your baby will be ready and when labor will begin. We can plan and we can prepare and we can have expectations, but at that point, we also have to acknowledge the things that are out of our control. One thing that is very often out of our control is *when* our baby decides that they're ready to be born.

GO-BAG READY-TO-GO!

In those last weeks and days before the expected birth date, it's important to make sure your ducks are in a row. That means having your conversations complete with any relevant insurance providers, any of those impacted by your expected leave from work, and any family or friends who you may want to be part of the birth experience. That doesn't always mean they're in the birthing room with you and your partner, or even in the waiting room. Often, it just means they're standing by during and after the birth to help out with things that can be difficult for any new parent – providing meals, doing laundry, or just being there to talk to.

However, among all those things is something you as a birth partner need to be extremely prepared for. Making sure your go-bag is packed, and making sure everything on your end is ready to go. Whether you're planning a birth at home, in a hospital, or at a birthing center, there's always things we need to make sure we need – even if it's not necessarily in one bag.

To help with that, we're going to list all the things you might want in your go-bag for general preparations, and then some ideas of what you might want packed for your other early responsibility, making the birthing room vibes absolutely immaculate.

THE GOOD-TO-GO-BAG

- A picture ID and insurance card or information.
- Multiple copies of your birth plan.

- Car-seat ready and installed! If at a hospital or birthing center they'll check to make sure you have one before you can leave.
- Essential toiletries like a toothbrush, contacts, bath items, and deodorant.
- Slippers and a bathrobe or nightgown for your partner (coziness first!).
- Extra long phone charger.
- Chargers for computers and other devices.
- Entertainment like books, journals, or tablets.
- Favorite snacks and drinks (if the vending machine doesn't have them).
- Cash or cards (for the vending machines or gift shops).
- Extra underwear
- Water bottle with a straw! It makes for easier hydration help while in labor.
- Extra hairbands in case your partner needs to put their hair up or keep it back.
- A bathing suit for a water birth (or in case your partner wants to shower and needs help being washed).
- A few pairs of comfortable clothes for you and your partner, as well as coming-home clothes for the baby!
- A postpartum kit (e.g. sanitary pads/big underwear for mom and possibly breastpads).
- And finally, baby nail clippers and a baby blanket.

THE POSITIVE BIRTH ATMOSPHERE BAG

- Essential oils of choice and a diffuser.
  Smells are a wonderful anchor and perfect for most any birth location - just make sure your provider approves first.

- Twinkling Christmas lights – they have battery powered ones! There's hardly anything better for crafting the perfect birth environment than warm lights bringing about a magical atmosphere.

- Battery powered candles.
  All the beauty of candles with none of the open flames - make sure to bring back-up batteries!

- Photos of loved ones, happy memories, or favorite pets.
  Anchors to help your partner stay calm and feel safe. These pictures can help them power through intense surges.

- Comfort items like a favorite pillow from home or a blanket.
  Not only do they have a familiar smell, but labor can go on for a long time and having some extra comfort for rest is vital to keep energy up!

- A Positive Affirmation Poster.
  A wonderful project that can be completed before the birth together, this poster or picture collage can have phrases from

relaxation scripts, encouraging mantras, and anything else to make sure your partner remembers just how strong they are!

- Portable speaker to listen to music out loud.
  Relaxing music can help the entire atmosphere of the room. Just like using music as a studying tool, music during birth can take your partner back to a moment they felt calm, giving them some immediate comfort.

- Headphones for your partner to listen to relaxation scripts.
  Headphones can be extremely valuable to listen to relaxation scripts and block any of the noise out helping your partner to focus inwards.

- Battery powered necklace fan (to keep your partner cool!).
  Keeping cool is so helpful as your partner is burning tons of calories during labor. This easy-to-use, unobtrusive fan is a lifesaver!

CHAPTER FIVE

THE BIRTH

WHAT YOU'RE GOING TO LEARN:

- The last-minute preparations for birth
- How to get you and your partner into the right mental state
- Getting the birth place settled to encourage comfort, confidence, and control
- Understanding the various positions to encourage labor and give birth
- A full breakdown of the first, second, and third stages of labor

Here we are. The moment we've all been waiting for is finally close. Labor could begin any day now. You're likely both waiting patiently, but also trying to distract yourselves from thinking about it too much. You might feel eager, anxious, even a little extra-fatigued because of that. Many mothers find sleep in the third trimester especially difficult and you might find yourself in the same boat.

There are a lot of unknowns too – your baby could arrive well-before 40 weeks or well after. Without an induction or a medical emergency that necessitates intervention, your baby ultimately decides when to get the ball rolling. Because of that, during these days and even weeks, you might find yourself standing by in a sort of daze, a mixture of nervousness and excitement in the calm before the storm.

We know it's easy to take that analogy as something negative, as if a storm is just inherently bad. But a storm, rain – that's birth and rebirth. A storm couldn't be more fitting for this next stage. The more time to think about something, the more time your mind can spin yarns on everything that could possibly go wrong. But this isn't rain on a wedding day, a storm can be beautiful if you're not lost in it, if you're prepared for it – hearing the rain patter on the roof, watching rivulets drip down the window.

And you *are* prepared for it. Even if you don't feel it quite yet, you've pushed yourself to focus your attention on birth and becoming the best birth partner you can possibly be. You've challenged yourself to be conscious of all that could happen in an effort to make sure what happens is a positive experience. You've put in the work to take on this amazing role and become better for your partner, your baby, and yourself.

So right now, shift your perspective on what the approaching storm is. You've already prepared, you know how to batten down the hatches if needed – you've studied, practiced, communicated, and you're both ready for this. Your perspective influences how you feel and act – and positivity is our goal.

You and your partner are ready. It's something beautiful, miraculous, refreshing, and rejuvenating. We can always be aware of the dangers or the risks without letting them cloud everything else. It's been a long road to get here, and you're equipped for what comes next.

And what comes next is...

THE FIRST STAGE OF LABOR

There are four stages of labor. The first stage of labor is often the longest stage and is broken down into three parts: **early labor, active** or **established labor**, and the **transition** to the second stage of labor. There are key markers that denote the transitions between labor stages, but it's important to know that most practices of hypnobirthing don't consider the first stage of labor until your partner is 4cm dilated, or when they move into established labor.

However, as birth partners, we have to be prepared and ready to go before that. Before the hospital, before the birth center, before the living room – everything needs to be set up. That's the first of your responsibilities.

HERE'S A FEW QUESTIONS TO ASK YOURSELF:

- Is your go-bag ready if you're going to the hospital? Is your car-seat installed?
- Are you keeping track of contractions?
  Sometimes Braxton Hicks contractions, or false-labor contractions, can show up infrequently in the third trimester. The reason they come is to prepare the uterus for real contractions – but sometimes their surprise or intensity can be mistaken for early labor contractions.
- Is your midwife up to speed on any changes?
- Is the tub already in place and waiting to be filled for a water birth?
- Have you put together or purchased a postpartum kit?

- Have the last calls to insurance providers been made and coverage confirmed?
- Is your job aware of how soon the potential upcoming leave could be?
- Do relevant family and friends know that labor is any day now?

If you answered yes to those relevant questions and any other ones you've thought of on your own, then you're ready for...

EARLY LABOR

This is the stage of labor often characterized by two things: 1) the baby telling your partner that they're ready to let this whole process unfold, and 2) the questions both you and your partner might find yourself asking – "Is this labor? Are we in labor?"

Whether or not your partner has experienced a lot of Braxton Hicks contractions during their pregnancy, actually knowing if these surges are the real deal or not can be difficult. For your own peace of mind, you can track the surges and their duration on a tracking app. If contractions are random and infrequent, they may be Braxton Hicks. However, if they are arriving at seemingly regular intervals, and more frequently, then it might be a sign of early labor.

That being said, surges between women aren't exactly consistent. Some might experience frequent surges for a few seconds at a time, others strong surges for over a minute but no discernable consistency. The three signs that labor is progressing, when it comes to surges, is that they continue to build in **duration, frequency,** and **intensity.**

With that in mind, whether it's early labor or not, you should treat it as though it is. Remind yourself of the golden rule of labor: to

encourage oxytocin and **discourage adrenaline**. That means in everything you say and how you project, make sure it's calm and in control so your partner is more likely to feel the same. If you're freaked out, she might be too. If you're calm, she more than likely will be too.

Another wonderful thing you can do during early labor is your very best distraction techniques. Keep things light and joyful. Many hypnobirthing experts say that when contractions begin, but your partner can still talk through them, then they should try their best to ignore them. You can help with that! Binge watch some shows on Netflix, laugh at a stand-up routine, eat a big, soul-enriching meal.

Also, try and be aware when tracking contractions that this information is more for you to be prepared, not your partner. Don't get too hung up on it and lose focus on your partner. Yes, you might need to time going to the hospital or alerting the midwife, but you don't necessarily need to be sharing constant updates. Remember, no matter where you are in labor, your partner needs to know she's in a safe space to encourage oxytocin, trusting that you will get her where she needs to be. Even if you are trying to be extra-precise with your surge tracking, or you feel frantic inside (it's completely normal), still try your best to maintain a level head and move forward step-by-step.

As you get things together around the house, to get ready to leave or to stay, check in on your partner - and at this stage like all the others, positive affirmations are welcome. Your goal is to try and read your partner without interrupting their focus or letting anything else - like their bag not being packed or a checklist of things to remember - cause any undue anxiety or stress.

On a physiological level, early labor is marked by the cervix opening (dilating) at about 4 cm. Remember, the uterus is contracting, and at this stage the surges can be further than 20 minutes apart, relatively light, and last for around thirty seconds. As the cervix gradually opens, some women will notice a clear pink or slightly bloody discharge from their vagina. This is sometimes referred to as the "bloody show" and is often the cervical mucus plug, which was formed early in the first trimester to protect the baby from bacteria and other things, being released.

This is another tell-tale sign that labor is progressing and the baby is on their way!

How long it lasts: The duration of early labor is extremely hard to predict. It can go on for hours or even days. Often, first-time mothers may experience a longer early labor and that's why you'll commonly hear that it's a good strategy to labor at home for this stage rather than going directly to the hospital or birthing center. If you go too early, sometimes they'll even turn you around and send you back home.

An exception to this is if your partner is receiving an induction, whether planned or unplanned. In this case, this early stage of labor will likely be getting started in the hospital or birthing center. The goal of the induction is to convince the body to kick-start the labor process and there is no set way of predicting how long that will take either.

What you can do: There's no telling what time of day early labor begins and how long it will last. However, this is also your very first practice round of using your new hypnobirthing techniques before the main event!

To help keep your partner comfortable during early labor, you can:

- Encourage steady breathing patterns
- Go on a walk together
- Draw a bath for them or a warm shower
- Diffuse oils
- Deliver water and food
- Give them a massage
- Play some relaxing music or recite relaxation scripts
- Help them to change labor positions

Which brings us to...

To apply counterpressure, use the heel of your hand and push with as steady, and strong a force as your partner requests. By the end, it can be a real workout for you – but obviously nothing compared to the marathon your partner is going through.

Many women actually elect to give birth on all-fours, but more on that soon!

SQUATTING & SUPPORTED SQUAT

One of the most common positions that pregnant women naturally find themselves going to is the squatting or supported squat position. Just like standing, the squat lets gravity do its thing and helps to open up the pelvis for the baby. Later on in the labor, as movement becomes more difficult, you might be the support for the squat as their legs get wobbly from the pressure and balance loss during surges.

Something else designed that can offer support and relieve leg pressure is a birthing bar, which many hospitals, birthing centers, and midwives attending home births might have available for your partner to use. But, if not, you're there for support!

SITTING & SITTING ON THE TOILET

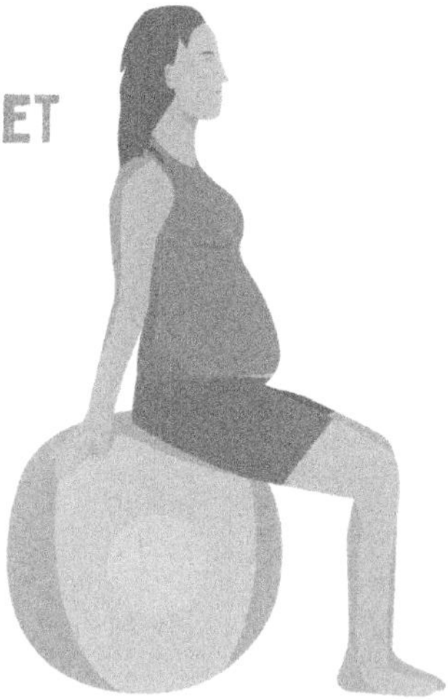

Sitting on a birthing ball, if available, can often help to reduce discomfort during labor. To add to that, it's also been said to induce labor and encourage it in the earliest stages – likely from the added help of gravity and opening of the pelvis. However, if a birthing ball isn't available, a number of our dads and their partners swear by the magic of the toilet. Somehow, the throne is not only comfortable, but the magic seat for encouraging a steady progression of labor.

Also, this provides the shortest trip for your partner's pee break!

WATER MOVEMENTS

Almost every position we named above can also be done, in some form, in a tub. Water tubs, even if not used for the birth, have often been regarded as wonderful during labor. The warmth naturally helps with comfort and the production of oxytocin, and you have great access to comfort your partner, give massages, or even sit in the tub alongside them should they ask.

And, with all these labor positions in your back pocket, it's time to move on to...

ACTIVE LABOR

In hypnobirthing, the first stage of established labor is referred to as the "Up Stage" for the exact same reason as the up-breathing exercise we went over previously. The "Up Stage" is marked by the uterine muscles drawing up, sort of like window blinds all tightening together, hitting the head of the frame, and then slowly unraveling back down. During this stage, you and your partner will get plenty of practice with those powerful up-breaths.

Active labor begins when the cervix has dilated to about 4cm (although some places have recently updated that to 6cm). The only way to check that accurately is for a doctor or midwife to perform a cervical examination. However, that examination is an extremely invasive procedure and many women elect not to have it done. Ultimately, knowing how open the cervix is doesn't help it open any faster. In fact, sometimes learning how dilated or effaced the cervix is (as it's the primary measure of labor stages) can cause more distress than it's worth.

If your partner has already gone through labor for hours or a full night, and already feels exhausted by the contractions, finding out they're only 5cm dilated rather than the 4cm they were hours before likely won't make them feel much better.

The other way to know how labor is progressing is through the contraction app that you've been using (remember: **duration, frequency, intensity**) and paying attention to your partner's breathing. Often, the move from early labor to active labor is marked by some changes you can actually observe. Your partner might become more inward, focused entirely during contractions. She likely won't be able to talk or engage during them at all, and you might notice a change in her breathing patterns too.

The contractions, getting more intense, can cause quick, successive breaths and it will be a tell-tale sign for you that she's experiencing a surge. In those moments, maintaining the up breathing is essential, but also difficult. What you can keep an eye out for is whether her breaths are staying deep and controlled. Typically, at the peak of a surge, breathing rates can increase, but by breathing with her, and showing gentle up breaths or breaths in and out through the mouth, to let the carbon dioxide balance out the overabundance of oxygen, can help her find her rhythm again.

However, as we mentioned, focusing on labor is what your partner is doing at the outset, but you have a different job as well – getting to your birthing location and...

"The days leading up to Zyair's birth; Rachel was following her same routine. She was having her normal practice waves (Braxton Hicks) daily, but nothing that was too alarming. The only noticeable change was her sleeping pattern. She was very uncomfortable and restless. Thursday morning at 3:44 am I called the midwife to give an update on Rachel because she was having a lot of waves (Hypnobirthing word for contractions). I was so tired that I forgot the midwife's name and I forgot to call back to give a second update. I'm guessing Rachel finally got comfortable on the couch and got some rest."

- Brion W. California, US.

"We did a lot of labouring at home, and Laura really drew on the Hypnobirthing tools that we'd learned and had a lot of contractions here at home. So we got to the hospital around seven centimetres dilated. And yeah, I mean, the midwives were great. The midwives are actually from the birth centre, so they're very much positive birthing advocates as well. She unfortunately didn't give birth in the pool at the time because there were issues with meconium and things like that. So we had to get out but from getting out of the pool to being on the bed, maybe 10 or 15 minutes later Willow was born, and she did it all without any pain relief. The room was set up with music, affirmations, and there was a photo of Laura's mom Maxine with us, you know, so we really got through it that way really. She was phenomenal."

- Ben G. Worcestershire, UK

SETTLING IN

Moving from early labor to active labor marks a definitive change in the atmosphere. While during early labor you both might have been asking, "is this labor?" – in active or established labor, you are absolutely sure that "this is labor." That newfound knowledge also means that your weeks and months of planning are about to be acted upon.

We know in movies that this stage is usually marked by a frantic rush to the hospital, but you absolutely **do not need to rush to the hospital**. In fact, remove the word "frantic" from your mental dictionary for now. You've planned, you've prepared, and now you're going to embody the calm that your partner is trying to maintain.

If you're having a home birth, the doulas and midwives should be alerted. If you're heading to the hospital or the birthing center, now is the time to help your partner into the car, make sure your go-bag and atmosphere bag are with you, (and the car seat is installed), and head that way safely and carefully.

If transferring for a hospital birth, you can do a few things to help on the way. For one, offering that she sits in the back of the car not the front to give her more space and make her more comfortable can help, as can packing a pillow and a cozy blanket. This is also a good point, especially on a long drive, for her to listen to her relaxation scripts or calming music. It might be a good idea to have headphones for that as you don't want to get too relaxed and meditative while driving.

That being said, if your partner seems comfortable, on the drive or the wait for the midwives and anyone else to arrive to your home, it might be a good time to take a moment to ready yourself. In order for your partner to be able to focus on her labor, you need to stay focused on preventing distractions. First and foremost, that means that you need to be taking care of *yourself*. Make sure you have food packed and you have your spare clothes and deodorant. It's important that you have what you need to make sure *you* are looked after too. In this next stage, the only way you'll be able to be the better birth partner, is if you're fed, hydrated, rested (enough), and mentally prepared.

When it all begins, the first thing to keep in mind is being the initial point of contact with whoever is involved. Conversation stimulates your partner's neocortex (or the thinking part of her brain) which makes her more likely to produce adrenaline – so the goal is to have her answer as few questions as she can. Often, she'll set the tone for how much she's wanting to speak, but your goal is to be the person who *can* answer relevant questions, and take the initiative to answer them when needed. This allows your partner to keep their focus on labor. Of course, there's a line to toe here, because you don't want to in any way be, or appear to be, controlling. But if you conduct yourself with respect for everyone involved, especially your partner, we know you'll be fine.

Once you check-in at the hospital or with your midwife, you can join your partner in the birthing or delivery room. When you get there, and your partner is either in the bed, or in some way comfortable with all she needs for the moment (whether food, water, a fan, entertainment, or otherwise), you can start to shape this room into the ultimate, atmospheric, birthing space. In all fairness, if you are having a home birth, there is a higher likelihood that some things are already in place – regardless, *now* is a good time.

One of the first things you can do is to turn the lights down or off. Women's bodies produce melatonin in the dark, and melatonin is essentially a hormone that "increases the power" of oxytocin. So, start off strong with that x2 bonus power-up. After that, continue to set up the room with everything you have prepared and, in the case of a hospital or birthing center, everything that is approved. String up lights, play music over a speaker, pin an affirmation board in your partner's line of sight, diffuse some essential oils (or put a few drops on a cloth for your partner to hold), and make everything for them as comfortable as possible. The guardian *and* interior designer of the cave!

Now, we can get back to...

> "When in labor with our daughter, my wife went into the hospital and declined everything including IV. She got into a squatting position and gave birth naturally, silent, and at peace. Our last two children came out in three pushes or less and my wife did not experience fear or pain."
>
> - Jacob C. California, US.

> "I felt I had a bit more of an active role and that I had more control around the contractions, for example and using massage to help relax Clemmie as the contraction happened, and then also leading the breathing through those contractions. It was my job to make sure we were counting through the breathing, and making sure that we were doing it together."
>
> - Simon H. Bristol, UK.

ACTIVE LABOR & THE TRANSITION

Your partner is settled in her ultimate birthing location. The basic check-in procedures are done: whether placing an IV, starting Pitocin, performing a cervical check, or nothing at all! And your partner is simply laboring away nicely by herself. This is where the techniques of hypnobirthing and the tools in your toolset are going to become invaluable.

As you move through your toolset, listening to your partner's needs along the way while considering their stoplights, always remember to underscore everything with a positive tone. Your partner may not need you to speak much during labor, but if she wants that gentle reassurance, keep your language positive: tell her she is incredible, tell her you love her, remind her of how powerful she is!

When women are in labor, the massive mixture of hormones can have them very emotionally susceptible – their body is looking for any threats, any reason at all to produce adrenaline, and you don't want that to happen. As you expand on being a point of contact, make sure nurses are aware that you'd prefer conversations on topics you're able to answer to be conducted out in the hall. Most midwives will do this already. But the small things like that allow your partner to focus all their energy where it's needed.

Near the end of the active labor stage is the **Transition Stage**, and with it comes the more intense and more frequent surges. They can last from 60 to 90 seconds and be powerful enough to take your partner's breath away – and, if they're standing, these surges may cause their legs to wobble or even give out. During this time, labor positions can help to reduce some of the intense sensations of the surges, but for the most part your goal is to help your partner ride the waves. Support her, hold her, give her positive affirmations.

This is the time where your partner might say something like, "I can't do this anymore. I've changed my mind. I'm not ready for this." This often happens because they get a surge of adrenaline just before the birth. It's a sign that the baby is very close. As birth partners, knowing this can make sure we maintain our positivity and support. Tell them they can do it, that they *are* doing it, and that they're doing great. The adrenaline at this stage can bring on fear, but encourage your partner through it.

Every surge is one step closer to the birth. Remind her of that, encourage her, and make sure she knows how strong and powerful she is. She can do this!

Your partner might also feel the urge to push at this stage and if that is the case, they or you, need to make the relevant healthcare provider aware. The urge to push is very often involuntary at this stage and the uterus will start to do so without any say from your partner. We're going to go over that in detail in the next section, in addition to what "pushing" and "coached pushing" is.

Finally, in active labor and throughout the birthing process, your biggest goal is to **be present** and **advocate** for your partner. Do your best to always make sure she's being heard and her wishes are respected. And if in the moment you still find yourself unsure how exactly to help, just be present. Be there.

You might feel a little overwhelmed, you might be nervous or suddenly blanking on how to properly perform a technique you thought might help. That's okay. Just be present. Not just physically, but emotionally – completely.

Hold her hand, stroke her hair, give her a kiss – if she doesn't want to be touched, give her space. Look her in the eye and tell her she's the most incredible human on this planet (because she is), and when you've told her once, tell her again. And if she doesn't want any talking or any noise, you're there with your energy – your presence is present. She can absolutely do this without you, but you can make it a heck of a lot easier.

Be there. Be present. Be her advocate. And stay positive!

How long it lasts: Active labor can last from four to eight hours or longer. Even if reading through all this makes it seem brief, it very, very likely won't be. On average, your partner's cervix will dilate roughly 1 cm per hour. That being said, we've had plenty of dads experience every variety of this. Some have had it where the cervix was 8 cm dilated for hours and just wouldn't budge. Some have had it where their partner was 6 cm dilated and then 10 cm within the next 10 minutes! Because of that variety, the transition stage often lasts between 15 and 60 minutes.

Whatever the pace, whatever the speed, whatever the baby decides and your partner's body encourages – the **Second Stage** begins at 10 cm dilated and 100% effaced.

What you can do: We know we've covered a lot of what you can do during active labor already, but this is absolutely the time where you put your hypnobirthing tools and techniques to the test. As a quick reminder of all of that, we'll list your toolset and a few other good things to remember below, starting with:

- Make sure the atmosphere for birth stays just right
- Ensure both you and your partner are fed and hydrated
- Breathing techniques (remember up-breathing for active labor)
- Relaxation scripts
- Use your B.R.A.I.N.
- Set anchors (use pictures, music, smells, and words to evoke memories)
- Be her continuity of care

TAKE A BREATH

We're moving into the big moment. Active labor and the transition stage marks the end of the longest stage of labor, and now we're on to the stage where you'll finally meet your baby. This can all go by in a flash, or it can feel like time stops – so however long this brief moment between the transition's end and the first push is, *take a breath*.

One breath in, one breath out. You're ready for this. Both of you are.

Let's meet your beautiful baby.

"I didn't like say anything or speak to her. Just the tape was on. All I had to do was if the tape stopped to play it again and she was just focused on the breathing and listening to the tape. And yeah, I think we got to hospital and about an hour and a half later, the baby was here, and the birth was over. It was like almost a perfect in terms of how she was just in the zone. I would say 'hold the handrail if you need me there,' but she was just in the zone, which is a completely different experience from the first one where we went on for about 16 hours and I think was a lot more painful for her. Whereas this one she was breathing through it and you could see she was just there really in the zone. It was actually quite magical to watch."

- Mike B. Pwllheli, Wales

"So we had a midwife in the room but she very much just sat at the end of the room and would occasionally come up and just make sure everyone was okay. But then it was just me and my wife. She was in the pool and I was very close, and I was massaging and watching her you know, breathe baby out and everything. I think the principles we took from Hypno birthing is that maintaining of calmness. And not thinking she's got to have drugs or she's got to be lying down or we've got to have someone with us all the time. It was having to trust for me to trust her that she knew her body and was responding accordingly."

- Adam S. Tunbridge Wells, UK.

THE SECOND STAGE (DOWN STAGE)

The second stage of labor is what hypnobirthing experts like to refer to as the Down Stage. This is where the breathing techniques we've learned change in order to facilitate the baby moving *down* from the uterus, *down* through the cervix, *down* through the birth canal, and out of the vagina. You can encourage those down breaths by doing them yourself or with a gentle reminder.

How long it lasts: The first stage of labor may have been the longest, but that doesn't mean this stage is always short. The second stage of labor can last anywhere from a few minutes to a few hours. Many first-time moms take longer in this stage, and the use of an epidural can also cause this stage to become longer.

What you can do: Your goal in this stage remains the same as it has been throughout the process – be present for your partner and be their advocate. The transition stage also means your partner will be able to move less easily between labor positions. That means that whatever position they find themselves in may very likely be the position they give birth in. However, sometimes there is the opportunity to experiment in between pushes to find the position that works best. You can help them into birthing positions like:

- Squatting or using a birthing bar
- Sitting (sometimes on a toilet – it's more common than you might think!)
- Kneeling
- On all fours or leaned over a bed/low support

- In a tub of water
- Lying on their back (often with their legs in stirrups)

With all that in mind, the biggest marker of the second stage is that it's now...

TIME TO BEAR DOWN

Just like labor, there is no set measure as to how many pushes it will take for your partner to birth the baby. However, it's important to note that hypnobirthing mothers don't "push." Just like "delivery" is a misnomer for "birth," many hypnobirthing experts prefer "birth process" over "labor" – women who practice hypnobirthing aren't encouraged to "push"; they are encouraged to **bear down** and **breathe**.

The word "pushing" immediately conjures up ideas of women purple in the face from holding their breath and contorting themselves to force the baby out. But just like during labor, their muscles still need oxygen and blood to function effectively. Caretakers can tell women to "push, push, push," until they're purple in the face too, but no push will be more powerful than the natural expulsion reflex of the uterus and birth canal. They are the muscles of the body quite literally designed for this.

During the transition stage of labor, we mentioned that women might feel the urge to push. That urge is often uncontrollable. If you watch a pregnant woman's stomach at this stage, when they feel that urge to push, you will literally see the surge of the uterus like a wave rising, cresting, and pushing down her body. It is remarkably powerful, and it happens naturally, without her input at all. Much like breathing, it's almost autonomic.

That being said, it's pretty uncommon for doctors to "let" moms bear down in any position they choose. Most will allow moms to bear down in whatever way they want at first but once the baby's head is visible, they, in some cases, force mom on her back. If birth on their back is something your partner does not want to do, this might be a moment where you need to speak up.

You can express things to the care providers like:

"We do not consent to..."

"Is my partner or baby in danger? If not, then..."

It's important to note that there is no evidence suggesting women should give birth on their back. It's only indicated if they need support in the form of operative birth, such as forceps or vacuum extraction, as it grants better access for health professionals. There are some cases where obstetricians can perform operative births with forceps while the pregnant woman is standing up or semi-recumbent, which offers more control to the women, but very few actually offer this as they seldom get experience with it.

That all being said, because the process is involuntary, trying to change positions that late can be extremely difficult. Trying to stop those powerful contractions pushing the baby down can be like trying to plug a dam. Often, we've heard stories from dads in hospitals where women were pushing and the nurses said, "wait, wait, the doctor isn't here yet!" At that point, trying to battle their own uterus is not only dangerous to the baby, but sometimes impossible.

In that same vein, "coached pushing" is the process by which a care provider will tell a pregnant woman when they should push, and when they should rest. Often, coached pushing is common enough to be a habit for many care providers, and even if they've been made aware that it isn't something that's a part of your birth plan - they're still human, and they might forget. If coached pushing isn't something your partner wants, this is the time where it might be up to you to remind your care provider and even tell them to stop if necessary.

In some cases, coached pushing is absolutely necessary, such as when a woman has received an epidural, and they can't feel where the baby is in the process. However, in a natural or unmedicated birth, coached pushing often increases the likelihood and risk of perineal tears. The reason this happens is that although we imagine the process of the baby being born as a path always moving forward – that isn't the case. The muscles of the uterus and all those involved in birth, alongside the complex mixture of hormones of the baby and the mother, are all communicating with each other through this stage. If the surges are allowed to push the baby down, as the mother breathes and bears down with those surges, then the baby may find a rhythm of two steps forward, one step back.

That one step back can frighten some care providers who are encouraging non-stop pushing during surges, but the slow descent is necessary to allow the muscles of the cervix and lower birth canal to relax and stretch. This time to stretch reduces the likelihood of tearing. Therefore, unless an epidural was used or another medication that greatly limits the mother's feeling during birth has been administered, coached pushing is not recommended by hypnobirthing experts. Instead, they prefer to go off the pace of the mother, and the baby – bearing down during the surges, breathing, and then taking the time to rest in...

THE MOMENTS BETWEEN SURGES

In the second stage of labor, surges still have a rise, a peak, and a fall. They don't last for the entirety of this stage, as there are breaks between them just like during the rest of labor and there's no way to predict how many surges it will take to birth the baby. With that, this can be among the most intense moments of the entire experience for your partner.

That's why it is absolutely essential that you're in a place to encourage her, to let her know how well she's doing, and tell her that she can get through this. One of the most difficult parts of the entire labor is right at the very end – what some women refer to as the "ring of fire." This is the point where the baby's head has descended enough to *crown* – to stretch the vagina and be visible from the outside. If you're watching, this might be the first moment where you see your baby's head and perhaps a little tuft of hair too!

However, this also represents the moment where the vagina, and the lower birth canal, are stretched the widest they will stretch and it can cause a severe burning sensation for your partner. As a simple rule of thumb, the longer your partner experiences the intensity and burning sensation of the "ring of fire," the more likely it is that she is *stretching* rather than *tearing.* The vagina evolved to "unfold" in a manner of speaking, to become the right size for the baby to be born. That being said, stretching can make the moment a lot harder, but the recovery and postpartum "easier," for lack of a better term. When tears and stitching occur, even everyday things postpartum, like peeing, can feel terrible.

This is also where the sounds your partner makes are likely the most prominent, intense, and primal– and this is the point where she might need you there the most. Let them squeeze your hand as hard as they have to. Let them feel comfortable making the sounds that feel natural to them. Because the "ring of fire" is considered by many women the most intense part of the entire experience, but it also represents the home stretch.

"She used what's called a TENs machine . Which was really helpful just for stimulation on her lower back as she continued to breathe. Interestingly, the surges were coming every five minutes from the start and they didn't really change for an hour. So she didn't really get those periods in between to rest . She was full on right the way through, but the TENs machine gave her an extra boost, and for a good couple of hours, that was enough to sort of help her through. Then after that passed, and the surges got more serious she moved into the birthing pool, which was excellent. And every time a surge came in every single five minutes there was inward breathing. Her picturing it and breathing in and really sort of concentrating was the thing that struck me. There was a real focus that she was doing to get the full breath in and then controlling and ignite every breath out."

- James C. Norwich, UK.

"We told the midwives before, when we did our birth plan that we ran through with them what we wanted. I was going to be hidden the birth lead. So we didn't want any disturbance. So the midwives weren't allowed to come in unless they need to do any monitoring, there was none. And we didn't want continuous monitoring. So they would literally just come in, monitor, and then and then go again. I sort of just gave them sign off for me to be able to relay any messages because in a hospital environment or any sort of care environment, I suppose she's the patient. So they talk to her directly. And it's nothing to do with me. And I'm not allowed to speak on her behalf, which is right. But Jess was adamant that she didn't want strangers coming up and asking her questions all the time. So she signed off on me being able to just relay those messages and things but it was just it was just her and me in the room - which was really cool."

- John H. Hampshire, UK.

"The birth really didn't happen as we expected, but many births don't! My wife had a planned c section due to complications later in pregnancy so we had a couple of days to prepare. She was nervous about the procedure, especially as she had to have another operation straight afterwards. I was pleased to use hypnobirthing techniques to reassure her and also to navigate our way through the operations and aftercare."

- Vijay J. Surrey, UK.

"We arrived at the birthing center at 10:11. Rachel was calm the whole ride. I thought she was sleeping for a moment. Once we got in the midwife took her to the back. After being checked, the midwife told me she was at a 3. In my head I'm like we're not having a baby no time soon. I was so out of it; I left the car seat at home and all the bags in the car. Shame on me!!! We make it back to the room around 10:45 pm. The midwife had given Rachel a few exercises to do, so the baby could get over her pelvic bone. Once I got back in the room; Rachel decided that she was ready to get in the jacuzzi tub. She had a moment where she told me to give her the "Peace cue" (Hypnobirthing cue for instant physical comfort). I figured maybe the exercises worked because the pressure waves picked up. But once again nothing major in my eyes. A lot of what I was looking for was based off my experience with Zayden. So, the nurse and I prepared the water, we had the orange bubbles going and her tracks were playing. After a few more waves, they told Rachel she should stand up. This was probably the only weak moment I saw. Her reply to them "I don't think I can get up". I told her after the next wave you will get up. Before that next wave, she changed her track to "Pushing Baby Out" (Hypnobirthing track just for pushing). In the midst of il all, she was able to pause and change a track on her phone. Once we got her to stand, within the next 2 waves Zyair made it into this world at 1:35 am. Almost one hour after her water broke!!!"

- Brion W. California, US.

> "It got to a stage where we know that they were thinking that because Rhian is so calm she can't be dilated enough yet, so it's probably going take a while but they thought they would check anyway. And then next thing you know, the midwife is like, oh, okay, I think Juno is going to be here in about an hour! Then an hour or hour and a half later she arrived and yeah, it was it was incredible! Even now, I think a month or so ago I played that anchor music track back to myself and it was so ridiculous, I almost started crying. It just brought back so much stuff and I was like well okay, let's not play that. Too much. Just leave that alone."
>
> - Laurie A. London, UK.

THE POSITIVE BIRTH PARTNER FAQS

1) How will I know if my partner really needs my help?

Reading your partner during birth can be an extremely challenging thing to do, but what it requires is your absolute focus. She's focused on the birth, you're focused on her. How well you know your partner beforehand can definitely come into play here, but it isn't the be-all-and-end-all.

Labor, as we've mentioned, can go on for a long time. During that time, so long as you're engaged, involved, and looking for ways to be of assistance and limit distractions, you'll find your role and the two of you will find a rhythm. It'll be unique, just like your baby, but you'll start to understand the ebbs and flows – when she needs water, when she needs a little support walking, when the nurses talking loudly nearby are breaking her concentration, you'll know how best to be the remedy.

2) What if a particular technique isn't working for us at all - like relaxation scripts or visualizations?

We mentioned before that what you want to bring to the birth is the whole toolset. Sometimes what you use won't be the right tool for the job, and sometimes a tool will work for a time but not later on. You bring the whole toolset so you have everything you need when the time comes. You have the knowledge, the techniques, and the counterpressure!

You have everything you need and you are ready - you just have to discern which tools are working and which aren't. But always remember your most valuable asset is simply being present and attentive to your partner's needs.

You do that, and the rest will work out.

3) What if labor isn't progressing?

Labor failing to progress is a common enough instance in birth for there to be a term attributed to it. There are a number of things that can impact labor progression but something important to know is that labor progression is a term based on standards, not on your unique partner and your baby.

However, with that said, the biggest impact on the progression of labor is the production of adrenaline. If your partner is feeling on edge, anxious, unsafe, constantly interrupted, annoyed, or unnecessarily worried when terms like "failure to progress" are tossed around; if they aren't allowed to move around, to try various labor positions, to be free in their own birth, then all of these things can have an impact.

In all of these cases however, it's important to use your B.R.A.I.N. Benefits, Risks, Alternatives, Instincts, Nothing. If your partner is there to consult with, see how they're feeling. It might be time to ask questions about what options are available to progress the labor, or it might be time to do nothing. The only thing to be sure of is that whatever happens next is up to you and your partner, it's a decision you make together and is not just something that happens to you.

4) What if I forget an item that was meant to help create the ideal birth environment – like twinkling lights or a speaker?

We're all human. Sometimes in a frantic rush to get everything together as we pack-up and go, we leave something behind. Even if you've planned everything down to the last washcloth, those final moments before departure can still have you leaving that one important thing on the counter or in the laundry bin. The bottom line, it's okay.

You're the birth partner that's right for the job and you're right for the job because you know how to adapt to it. If you don't have something vital, make do with what you have. If it's absolutely essential, maybe reach out to a friend or family member. Have them stop by your home and pick-up those twinkling lights or phone charger.

The most important thing is not to let small things affect you, and in turn affect your partner. If she's upset by something missing, reassure her that you're solving it and it's going to be okay.

5) What if my care provider isn't respecting something in our birth plan?

Often we don't know who our care providers will be during the birth process and ultimately the birth. Sometimes one provider agreed to something on our birth plan while the other has a different opinion. All providers are different, and what they believe or practice during birth might be different too.

The important thing is to make your birth plan known. Ideally, you will have gone over most of these points with your care provider before the actual birth and labor. However, if it happens to be during the actual birth process, then you will still be prepared to articulate you and your partner's preferences. If your care provider isn't respecting something on your birth plan, don't be afraid to speak up. Standing up for you and your partner's hopes and goals for birth doesn't inherently mean starting conflict, it just means making something known. Oftentimes care providers go about their typical routines and need reminders if your birth plan is in contrast to that.

That won't always mean they'll object, it may simply be that they weren't aware. However, if it does seem like a point of contention, try your best to bring any disagreements away from your partner so that she can remain focused on birth and producing oxytocin.

"We did have some issues prior to the labour, but not physical issues. Thankfully Willow was fine the whole way through, but certainly the lead up to the due date, there was lots of talk of induction and, you know, the placenta giving out. So we had a really difficult consultancy. Just before the due date, the doctors were talking about booking us for an induction and we knew we didn't want that - we wanted to have a natural birth. The experience of being consulted over an induction was just so backwards in the way that they just want to get you to a date and it feels like you're on a conveyor belt. We'd done a lot of research about the statistics of inductions and what can potentially happen, the risks and benefits of everything. We really pushed back but yeah, it wasn't the best consultancy unfortunately as they started talking about things like still birth, and even the quote which makes us shudder even now when the doctor said: "you know you'll have a dead baby in your tummy if you don't go through with this." It was horrendous. And for someone who potentially hasn't done the research that is really frightening. You know, it was frightening for us but we had the back-up of the stats and we've done the research through hypnobirthing."

- Ben G. Worcestershire, UK

6) My partner asked for an epidural that wasn't in her birth plan? What do I do?

Sometimes birth plans really are just guidelines. We talk about everything we want and everything we don't, but in the moment, things change. In the moment, we feel differently - and that's okay.

There's nothing wrong with getting an epidural and there's nothing wrong with changing a birth plan on the spot - so long as it's a choice you and your partner are making, not something you are being told to do.

If your partner adamantly didn't want an epidural beforehand, but is asking for one during the birth, try your best to gently confirm that she is absolutely sure. Whatever the decision, decisions make for a positive birth experience. Autonomy. Control of choices. The various options for birth and pain management aren't there to make anyone feel guilty for using them, or feel bad about going against a plan. They are there to help in the event they're needed.

7) What if my partner doesn't want my help?

After going through the process to prepare, to practice, to be there to help - you can't always predict how your partner will react in the moment. Sometimes prior relationships play a role, sometimes other life situations come into effect.

Whatever the case, you still have a role to play in birth and your baby's life.

If your partner doesn't want to use the tools or techniques you practiced together, still try your best to be present and attentive. If there's any harsh words, try to brush them off and move forward.

8) What if the care provider isn't respecting my partner's informed consent?

Informed consent is absolutely essential in all aspects of life and it's just as essential in birth. Your partner should always feel in control of her own body and feel respected throughout the process. A care provider should *always* ask before performing any invasive procedure and should *always* wait for your partner to respond before proceeding. If at any moment that does not happen, don't be afraid to speak up.

Your partner should never feel like things are happening to her without her say so, and if she is unable, or for any reason can't say so, be her advocate. Again, this doesn't necessarily imply conflict, but it does imply being firm in how important that consent is. Again, this can come back to a provider's "routine" – but in this respect especially, routines need to change. For any event that is especially impactful, don't be afraid to escalate the issue to higher levels - even if it comes after the birth and stay.

9) What if the baby has to go to the Neonatal Intensive Care Unit - NICU?

It's impossible to predict everything that will or could happen in a birth, that's why it's important to speak with your partner before the actual birth about possibilities – even sometimes the more difficult ones to talk about.

The NICU is designed to help babies who need intensive care. It's not something that any couple wants to have in their birth plan, but it's something every couple should be aware of. In the event of a complication, or most commonly a premature birth, your baby might be taken to the NICU for observation, procedures, and assistance.

If that happens, one of the most important things you and your partner have to decide on is whether or not you follow. It's likely she will be unable to, but you most often go and observe everything happening, giving your partner updates when possible.

10) How do I react when they say an emergency caesarean birth is necessary?

"Emergency" is the operative word here. This caesarean birth isn't planned or even expected. If it happens, your partner might be very understandably overwhelmed. Even if you are too, the best thing you can do for your partner is maintain positivity. Encourage her that she can do this, that it's going to be okay.

Our words impact our perspective. Whatever doubts we have, it's not the time for them. Caesarean births are common and even when unexpected, lead to safe and healthy births.

That being said, emergency caesarean births are still situations where using your B.R.A.I.N. is absolutely essential. Benefits, Risks, Alternatives, Instincts, Nothing. *Why is caesarean birth necessary? Are there alternatives? What happens if we wait?* In these moments, as dire as they seem, make sure you don't feel forced into this decision. Make sure you can have your questions answered and your concerns acknowledged.

"An hour or two after the birth I remember I was talking to my mother on the phone holding our baby and Jessica got up to go to the bathroom. And I could see her and all of a sudden she collapsed and feinted. And I was on the phone with my mom. I was like Jessica just collapsed. I gotta go. And I went and just like a movie had to pull the little string in the bathroom that calls the emergency forces over and so Jessica had a really bad postpartum haemorrhage. Oh, pretty serious one actually. And so they rushed her out to give her blood. That was a very traumatic and that was probably the scariest moment of my life. I was holding my child watching Jessica, you know, and it was just like it all happened so fast. I just prayed and I just watched and waited in total shock. I couldn't even say anything the doctors made sure I was sitting down as they thought I was gonna faint with the baby. But I mean deep down I had this peace that it was gonna be okay. And then all of a sudden she came to and it was fine. She had lost a lot of blood and that was a pretty traumatic event, which also made us glad that we were in an environment like that. And there's all sorts of reasons why that happened. But it was just a reminder that things, unexpected things, can happen. And so it's always important to prepare your mind."

- Ben L. Arkansas, US.

"Through the education of the courses, we learned that we can take our time. You can refuse anything they want to do to you any point. Have your own birth plan and make sure they learn it. If you feel you have to, just intervene and make sure that you're the ones who get to do what you want to a certain extent. Because I do think they were very much sticking to a 'traditional script' in the sense that Luna went from cervix to vagina in about half an hour, but was crowning for three hours. So Emma did need and was being encouraged to push and push and push and nothing was really working. At one point, they said to her, if nothing starts happening, we'll have to call an ambulance."

- Joe S. Tonbridge, UK.

From the hospital side I felt ready. I'd been given the tips on when to push back with doctors. You can ask why, you can say no! It was empowering! Beatrice's birth was so premature, and when she was in intensive care, rather than just sit back I asked what the jargon means. "Can I get some background on that?" It helped massively to reassure and also understand exactly what was going on."

- Lewis J. Somerset, UK.

> We opted for a home birth. We both looked at each other and smiled rather than those last minute alarm bells. We knew it would be a few hours until real labour would happen. We drew all the blinds in the house, had fairy lights on, and watched sitcoms, and then went for a nice walk - just to keep super positive energy going on in the house. Around 12 hours after those waters breaking, the surges started. Alex went into this state where she wasn't aware that I was there. Minimal noise, dim lights. Letting her body do what it's naturally designed to do. It was quite emotional seeing her go through that. Once the contractions reached a certain point, I called Labour Line at midnight and ALL the midwives were out at birth. I was trying to provide food and drink for Alex, which was difficult. She just wasn't hungry or thirsty. Unfortunately we had to be transferred to hospital because she was incredibly tired from a very long labour and the surges had worn off..., but because we went through hypnobirthing we knew what to expect, and how I could communicate and keep other 3rd parties distanced to keep Alex in control of her birth.
>
> - Ben H. Hampshire, UK.

INTERVENTIONS & EXPECTATIONS

Before we move on to the moment we've all been waiting for, we have to acknowledge one thing about birth – it doesn't always go to plan. As much as you prepare, as much as you read, as many classes as you take, as intently as you study about the physiological needs of the body and set up the absolute perfect birthing environment for your partner – we just can't predict everything that might happen. Even after getting the best possible support team around you and checking all the possible hypnobirthing boxes, unforeseen things can still happen that require intervention.

- Health issues might impact pregnancy and birth
- The cervix might be obstructed
- The pelvic floor might be too tight
- The baby could be in a difficult position to allow for physiological progression
- The labor goes on for an extremely long time
- Your partner might want pain relief
- Unforseen or dangerous complications might occur

As we said from the beginning, a positive birth isn't about everything going to plan, it's about feeling in control, empowered, and understanding the choices presented to us. Interventions can have a negative connotation, but their existence is still an amazing feat of medical ingenuity. That we can birth babies safely who might otherwise have resulted in stillbirth or harming the mother is an amazing achievement. We can be thankful, even relieved by these amazing innovations in birth – but that still doesn't negate the evidence that birth is a natural process. In that way, physiological practices for birth should be the norm. Birth is not always a medical emergency, and interventions should be choices made by you and your partner, not decisions thrust upon you by care providers.

We don't need to spend nights staring at the ceiling focusing on it, but we do need to open our minds to the idea that our birth might not go according to plan. We need to, as a team, understand the options available so that we can make the best decisions possible in the moment – and feel confident that *we* made those decisions. Only if we do, can *any* birth feel like a positive experience. Whether it be natural, caesarean, VBAC, water birth, a planned or unplanned induction; birth at a hospital, at a birthing center, at home; birth in a Hazmat suit, on a plane, over video chat, or even on the phone while in the car frantically trying to fight through traffic – *your* birth *can* be a positive experience.

You and your partner will have done the homework, you will have had the conversations, and you'll be ready to make the decisions. So, without further ado...

ALLOW US TO INTRODUCE

Your beautiful new baby. After however many surges it takes, from whatever position your partner decides, once the baby's head comes out, the rest of their body typically follows shortly after. But with their birth, labor is still not over yet.

THE THIRD STAGE (THE GOLDEN HOUR)

Welcome your beautiful baby to the world. They've arrived.

There is no easy way to predict which position your partner chose to give birth in, or to predict if they had an epidural, were unmedicated, received a caesarean birth, or anything else. But, regardless of the manner in which they gave birth, and where they happened to be, barring an emergency, the next stage can feel familiar across the board.

Once your baby has arrived, the first thing you want to hear is their voice. Their cry. Sometimes they'll come out crying, but other times they won't. Because their lungs are still filled with a lot of amniotic fluid, sometimes mothers can pat them on the back to help encourage their breathing.

If the umbilical cord is wrapped around their neck, what's called a nuchal cord, a doctor, midwife, or even the mother will simply unwrap the cord however many times it was tied. Nuchal cords can sometimes be dangerous as they can block the airway, but keep in mind that at the beginning, the umbilical cord is still helping your baby to "breathe." In other words, they look more dangerous than they are.

After that is done, however, hypnobirthing encourages that the mother be given the baby immediately for skin-to-skin contact. This is the start of "The Golden Hour."

How long it lasts: The third stage of labor is marked by the birth of your baby and technically comes to an end when the placenta is birthed afterward. This stage can often come with an amazing sense of relief as your partner is finally able to hold your new baby. We'll get into what exactly happens next in a moment, but the placental birth often happens between thirty minutes to an hour after the birth – sometimes longer!

What you can do: During this stage, you can hopefully breathe a sigh of relief as well. Labor is not over, as the birth of the placenta is still impactful, but it is often less intense for most women because they are finally holding the baby in their arms.

That being said, one of the first things you can do is understand the importance of...

THE PLACENTA & THE LIFELINE

As your partner holds your newborn baby, the baby will still be connected to them by the umbilical cord. The umbilical cord at this stage, is in the process of a transition. At the time of birth, the umbilical cord still holds nearly 30% of the newborn's blood, which is why delaying the clamping of the umbilical cord is greatly encouraged.

Delayed cord clamping should be the standard of care, but some hospitals still practice the clamping and cutting of the cord immediately. However, it's dangerous to do so as it can decrease birth weight, lower blood volume, and lower hemoglobin concentration, which can affect iron stores throughout the first year.

With that in mind, it's a good idea to make sure your healthcare provider knows that you want to delay the cord clamping until you can see that the umbilical cord is no longer pulsing with blood and turns pale. After that, we greatly encourage you to do the honors of cutting the cord. Just keep in mind that the Wharton's Jelly, the thick coating that keeps the blood vessels within the umbilical cord safe, is some thick stuff. It might take some doing to cut through it!

However, cutting the cord also brings up what happens to the placenta. Often, the reason for cutting the cord in a hospital is two-fold: 1) to have the baby free so that the nurses can perform Apgar measurement and tests – 2) so that the doctor who performed the birth can "deliver" the placenta.

The placenta, just like your baby, will birth itself naturally. That can take up to an hour or sometimes longer, but most often it will happen. However, after the umbilical cord is cut, doctors will often tug on the cord to release the placenta from the endometrium of the uterus. This is a common practice in many hospitals and will likely happen if you don't make it known that it's something you don't want. Just like coached pushing, the dangers of tugging on the umbilical cord to release the placenta are similar to peeling a scab. Only, the placenta is a lot larger. With that, the various points of contact where the placenta were latched to the inner lining of the uterus can cause hemorrhaging if they are pulled too hard or too early.

The placenta was firmly attached for good reason, after all. Something else that might happen, especially in the case of something like a velamentous cord insertion (where the cord attaches to the side rather than the center of the placenta), is that the umbilical cord could detach only, also putting the mother at risk of excessive bleeding.

The reason we bring this all up is that patience will help the placenta birth naturally, and reduce the unnecessary risk of tugging on the cord to deliver it.

COME HERE, LET ME HOLD YOU

It's also very likely that you and your partner won't mind waiting through this third stage of labor. This is finally the moment where your partner can hold the baby and begin to bond. But the value of the Golden Hour and skin-to-skin contact extends beyond that. The Golden Hour is vital because it can help encourage:

- Temperature regulation
- Breathing for the baby
- Initial breastfeeding
- A massive rush of hormones
- Did we mention bonding?

The Golden Hour can go on for as long as your partner wants. The placenta birth will likely happen sometime during this hour, but it doesn't inherently mark the end of it. These first moments with the baby can be truly beneficial for both the health of them and your partner, and just magical in general.

During this time, your goal is to make sure the birth environment is maintained - that means quiet conversations, low lighting, keep music playing if it is, and anything else to maintain the calm, peaceful, and safe atmosphere. This is the environment your baby has been born into, and all of those things will help them to feel calm and relaxed too. This encourages them to bond, stay relaxed as your partner is relaxed, and namely not be afraid of this new world they've just joined. That's a lot of unfamiliar all at once!

But after your partner has held the baby, it's equally important for you to get time to hold the baby as well. In just the same manner, the Second Golden Hour as we like to call it should involve skin-to-skin contact where your own oxytocin levels can surge just from holding, smelling, and caring for your beautiful newborn. In the event of a caesarean birth where your partner is unable to hold the baby first, a great way to make them feel safe in this new and strange environment is skin-to-skin contact with you. Not only will your oxytocin surge, but theirs too - especially when they hear a familiar voice!

A WELL-EARNED REST

After the hour is up, a few routine processes are likely to start happening if they haven't begun already. Among the first is the mother being stitched up if they experienced a tear during delivery. This stitching, even with a local anesthetic, is sometimes said to be the most painful part of the entire experience for many mothers as their entire pelvic area and pelvic floor is extremely tender after the birth. This is sometimes because women don't receive enough local anesthetic or epidural top-ups.

With that in mind, though you might find yourself distracted by your new baby, still, try to focus on being there for your partner. This is still a stage of labor, and they still need you. It's very important to advocate for the right amount to be given, or ask the provider to stop and only continue if a full dose has been administered and the woman is comfortable. Often, health professionals don't give the full dose just in case more is needed later – but barring other concerns, best practice is that the full dose should be given rather than saving it up for 'if' situations and the woman being in pain.

Other ways you can advocate for your partner is to make good use of your "drawbridge." Think carefully about who, if anyone, you want to invite into this space. You are both getting to know your baby and they're getting to know you. Sometimes, surrounding yourself with a moat can be really nice. Visitors can wait!

In the case of a water birth, this is also likely the time to get out of the tub – as it's very likely getting cold now for both the mother and baby. Leave clean-up for the moment, but make sure that there is an extra layer of blankets or towels to ensure the baby is warm and dry for skin-to-skin – and just remember that you're still trying to limit distractions overall. That might also mean delaying the announcements or calls to family just yet. But for now, just take things slow.

Maintain the calm you've been encouraging this entire time, and most of all – enjoy the well-earned rest while holding your beautiful newborn. You've all been remarkable, and you've all more than earned it.

"One thing that's really stuck with me is that if we had another, Lucy feels really confident that natural will be the way forward again, and I think I will be more attuned to the birth next time, and we'll do it together again."
- James C. Norwich, UK.

CHAPTER SIX

BEYOND THE BIRTH

We said at the beginning that every birth has the potential to be a positive experience and we firmly believe it. There is no way for us to guess the kind of birth you and your partner wanted to experience, but if you were able to communicate; if you were able to have the questions you asked, answered; if you were able to take on the experience as a team, then you did everything you needed to, which is more than enough!

Sometimes the plans we have for birth don't pan out exactly as we imagine them. Sometimes interventions are necessary for the safety of your partner and your baby – and that's okay. That's exactly why they're there in the first place. But we hope that everything that happened during the birth was a result of the choices you made together.

After the birth, it might seem like you won't need to use your *birth positive toolset* or the other techniques of hypnobirthing – but our dads have found that not to be the case. In fact, many of them have relayed a lot of creative uses for a multitude of hypnobirthing practices beyond the birth – and, before we leave, we'd like to share a few with you.

ON HIGH ALERT

In those first few hours, days, and weeks after birth, you might find yourself on high alert. It's a natural response, something instinctual as if a switch flipped in your head – "I'm pretty sure everything is a threat. Yep, the entire world. It's a threat."

You look at your baby and feel this overwhelming urge to keep them safe. In some ways, that urge can impact our ability to bond with our baby. We're so focused on their safety that our minds bombard themselves with questions like:

Are they breathing okay? Is it normal for their genitals to be swollen? Why won't they stop crying? Is this diaper too tight? Is that person we just walked by sick? Is my baby going to get sick? Am I supporting their head enough? Could they suffocate with that blanket? Are they okay in the backseat? Is this road too bumpy for the stroller?

All of these small or big worries can make it so we don't ask ourselves other questions like – *am I spending enough time just being with them?*

Just like you were during labor for your partner, the first thing you need to be for your baby is present. In a lot of ways, by focusing on safety and worrying about their wellbeing, you are being their advocate. But remember what we said about doctors and nurses thinking in the short-term? About their focus being on health and everything physiological rather than the experience?

ALLOW YOURSELF THE FREEDOM TO LIVE THE EXPERIENCE OF BEING A NEW DAD.

You are going to keep your baby safe. Even if you make mistakes, as all parents do. Something that helped a lot of our new dads was hearing that "newborns are designed for new parents." They feel so fragile, but they're a lot sturdier than you think.

Allow yourself to be present with them. Bonding isn't easy; it can take time. But taking that time is what will encourage the oxytocin in your brain to help you out. It will encourage the prolactin to make you more patient when you're exhausted at 3 am changing another diaper. Being present is the physiological boost your brain needs to help you bond with your baby. It won't always happen right away, but if you give it time, the connection you build will be unlike anything else.

EMBRACING A WHOLE NEW WORLD

The first hours, days, and months with your new baby are always unique. No matter how many you've had, from two to twelve, every baby has their own character that shines through early on. They might be the deep-sleepers, they might be the constant-eaters. They might cry all the time, they might hardly make a peep until the hunger really strikes. In that way, embracing this time with your baby is about empathizing with just how fresh and new to the world they really are.

However, it's not only the new baby that you're looking out for as a birth partner, it's your partner too. In those first months after the baby is born, what many call the fourth trimester, your partner's body has been through the wringer. They got through the marathon, the 15-round bout, and now, they need your help.

With that, don't be afraid to get your hands dirty. Change the diapers/nappies, become an expert at it. Time yourself and beat records. When your baby cries at night, and your partner is clearly exhausted (maybe even hiding under the covers), try your best to rock them back to sleep. If your partner does the nighttime feedings, do the nighttime changes. If taking shifts helps, stay a team. Pick up around the house, cook, clean, bring your partner some fresh water or a snack. Do whatever you can to support your partner as they battle with an exhausted body and hormones trying once more to achieve homeostasis. More than all of that, keep an eye on them. However the birth turned out, keep out for signs of PPD and if you find yourself on the receiving end of emotional outbursts, try not to take any of it personally.

As you read that, it might have gotten you worried for how life with a newborn might be. It also might have had you ask: *what about me?* You're tired too, after all.

That's the tricky balance to strike, but these things also aren't mutually exclusive - they just require communication. You and your partner are still a team and you can still lean on one another just as you did during the birth. But that only works if you're honest with one another. Pay attention to how you're feeling - be open about concerns or doubts or anxieties - don't bottle them up. You and your partner can bond over the challenges and the joys of living with the new boss in the house. That said, the only way you can be the better birth partner is if you take care of yourself first. And sometimes, the best way to do that is to reach out for help.

If friends and family offer to help, don't be afraid to say yes. Ask them to do practical things - send or bring food for you both, hold the baby while you have a shower, put a wash load on - it'll help you feel less stressed about keeping on top of those things and can also help you to be more present with your partner and baby.

Lean on your care providers. They are there for you and your baby, so don't hold back if you need to talk about anything - especially for questions concerning PPD.

Keep elements of your birth alive - put on the smell you had during labor, listen to your playlists again, or look at pictures as all of them can cast your memory back to that happy time of meeting your baby. All joys and good feelings still bring about oxytocin - not only will that help you to enjoy the time, but it will also encourage baby bonding.

Finally, remember that babies cry to communicate. The problem is a lot of the time we hear a cry we immediately think, "sad" or "hurt." On the rough days, we practically hear the cries saying "you're not good at this." It's not true. Those doubts and anxieties are in your head, and if your baby is relentlessly crying and you're flat-out exhausted, take a minute. Walk around the house, get your bearings, and take a breath.

You've got this.

Take it slow, take it day by day. Go easy on yourself. Play with them, feed them, bond with them, and spend time with them. Take any time you can to get to know how they're starting to see the world as they barely crack their eyes open, and you'll better understand your place right by their side and your partner's side.

"I think certainly the calm breathing has been useful post birth. You know, because it can be stressful, having a baby and certainly in public areas if she's having a bit of a scream, just staying calm. Me and Laura I think make a great team in that sense, and we were during labour too, and that is what it's about. You know, we don't kind of get panicky about it, because ultimately that's going to panic Willow."

- Ben G. Worcestershire, UK

"It's all around breathing deeply and then you hold it, and that's really useful, especially when you're having a bad day and the kids are playing up or whatever. You don't respond immediately because you hold that breath in, and that gives time for you to become calmer and to reflect more on what you're about to say."

- Simon H. Bristol, UK

"Claire's used some of the tracks to sleep better, actually. I remember there were times after the baby was born where Claire wasn't able to sleep. It was probably partly down to being overtired and all of that. And I know that she's listened to some of the tracks since birth to help her relax and fall asleep more easily."

- Adam R. Brighton, UK.

"We often use a lot of techniques still, especially the breathing exercises and visualisations. They're brilliant for many day to day situations!"

- Vijay J. Surrey, UK.

REMEMBERING WHAT YOU LEARNED

Something that's underscored by the practices and techniques of hypnobirthing, that we haven't mentioned yet, is patience. In everything we've gone over, every action and reaction, whether using your B.R.A.I.N., reciting relaxation scripts, or simply breathing – they all take and teach patience.

Hypnobirthing teaches us to think first and speak second. It encourages us to take that moment to process our feelings before letting them explode out unfiltered. There is perhaps no time in your life where patience is more important than life with a newborn. We don't mean to say it's inherently overwhelming, but we'd be lying if we said it wasn't. Waking up for late night changings, trying to console any non-stop crying, attempting to give your partner a break when you desperately need one too – it can be a lot. And in those moments, the practices of hypnobirthing can still help you.

We outlined the chair of positive birth – we said it required trust in your partner's body and your baby, calmness and relaxation, education and knowledge, and confidence and control. In these first days, weeks, months, years, and beyond with your baby – you'll need all of that once more.

You need **trust in your partner** to know that during the fourth stage of labor, they are recovering and repairing. There is no set time for that recovery, and their body will let them know what the new normal is. But you can trust that it will recover. To help in that recovery, you'll be there to provide support. You'll let them know that they will feel better, that you'll both learn more each day, and that any emotions they feel or thoughts they think can be shared with you.

You need **trust in your baby** that they are still growing at their own pace. They are learning and discovering new things each day. There are milestones for progression, but those are statistics based on averages, and your baby is still unique. You'll be there to support their neck until they find the strength to themselves, to sing them silly songs when they're upset, and to take care of them when they're sick.

To do all of that for your baby and your partner, you'll need **calmness and relaxation.** You'll need to know how to respond to things one at a time, to take on new challenges one at a time, even when they feel like they're piling on. You need to understand the value of your own mental health and wellness – that sometimes you do need to just step away for a moment to gather yourself. You need to let yourself know that you can relax, that you don't have to be constantly working or doing something to feel your worth. You deserve the same love as you give your baby and partner.

To understand how best to help your baby and partner through these new experiences of parenthood, you need **education and knowledge.** It's not a given that you'll know the best practices to help your baby through teething, to know how to wean them off breastmilk, and incorporate solid foods. It's not inherent that you'll know the signs of PPD in your partner or yourself, and are able to act upon it before it starts to affect your relationship.

And you need **confidence and control** to understand that you are a good father. You might not always have the right answers, and like everyone you will make mistakes, but you can be confident in the fact that you're trying your hardest. You are doing your very best each day for your partner, your baby, and yourself – and that's enough. And you need to understand when things are within your control, and when you need to relinquish the idea that you can control everything. You can control how you respond to situations, but that doesn't mean you can control the situation.

To make each of the legs of that chair strong, you will likely incorporate the tools in your toolset. You might need to practice those **breathing techniques** when you feel overwhelmed. You might read **relaxation scripts** to your baby to get them to sleep, or to your partner as a meditation to slow things down. You'll always use your **B.R.A.I.N.** when making decisions about your baby's health – about medications and treatments, or simply new trips and experiences. You might redesign your home to incorporate meditation and encourage a **comfortable environment**. It might even encourage you to see how good something as simple as a clean house can feel. You'll **set anchors** in the form of pictures, smells, and amazing memories created by moments with your new family. And finally, you'll be their **continuity of care**, as you're always the one they can rely on to love them and care for them.

By combining the four chairs of a positive birth, and applying the hypnobirthing techniques you've learned to your own path and journey forward as a father, you'll be able to start...

> **"Our baby Rune just smiles all the time. I am 99% confident that's because of how positively minded we were during the birth and how he came into the world."**
> - Ben H. Hampshire, UK.

EMBRACING A POSITIVE LIFE

There can be a lot of pressure to be the best possible parent in the world. When it's all still theory, when you're not actually living the day-to-day, we've actually discovered something interesting. Most of us were far better parents *before* we had babies.

We had all these imaginings of what we would do and what we absolutely wouldn't do. We'd teach them baby sign language, read to them for hours a day, never let them watch TV or have a tablet in the back seat. We make those declarations to ourselves, or even out loud – and when at any point we fall short, we feel guilty, or feel like a failure. But you shouldn't and you're not. When we daydream about the kind of parent we'll be, we often ignore all the other aspects of life we'll have to balance alongside being a parent. The reality can be more difficult, but often because our ideals are making them so.

With that, give yourself a break.

The tools and techniques of hypnobirthing are designed for birth – what birth actually is, not what we like to believe it to be.

Throughout this book, we've tried to give you an honest impression of the experience of birth. That experience isn't always easy, and many births, no matter how hard or how much you prepare, can still be difficult. But the goal of hypnobirthing is seeing the positive in whatever experience you have.

That might be revisiting the past, and recollecting the things that made it so hard before you knew what you know today – or it might also mean being optimistic about a future that you have no control over.

The world exists as it is, the good and the bad – but we choose how to frame that world. We choose how we see it. That doesn't mean choosing to be ignorant to things we don't like, but it does mean choosing what we'll let affect us. Hypnobirthing is about your partner having the belief in herself that she can do something she might be terrified to do, and it's about you believing that you have the power, the ability, and the confidence to make the best of any situation.

Even if the birth didn't turn out how you wanted, even if life doesn't turn out how you expect, you can still choose how you react. Yes, you could always focus on all the things you missed out on, maybe that idyllic water birth at home – or you could focus on all the things you actually have – a beautiful, healthy baby and a partner who was in control of her experience. Hypnobirthing is about embracing the good, and accepting the things we can't control, but finding the good in them anyway.

And with that, we leave you to find your own way to embrace a positive life with your new or perhaps just slightly bigger, family. But before we go, we'd like to do two things.

The first is that we want to encourage you to sign up for a hypnobirthing class if you haven't already. Even with as much as we packed into this book to lay out the techniques of hypnobirthing and a path to positive birth, there's nothing better than direct, in-person, or virtual instruction catered to your unique birth journey.

The second is that we'd like to invite you to join other dads and birth partners who are on the same journey as you, many of whom you've heard from in this book, to talk to about your own experiences. For more blog posts, step-by-step guides, reflections, and conversations with a community of dads who are experiencing all of this at the same time as you, check out our website at www.daddilife.com and join the community at www.facebook.com/daddilife

From there, you'll have access to even more information on hypnobirthing and its history, as well as more amazing tips and tricks for fatherhood. Join us in the journey, conversation, and community. We're happy to have you!

OUR GIFT

ACKNOWLEDGEMENTS

ACKNOWLEDGEMENTS

A massive thank you as ever to the DaddiLife team - David, Emilie and Jon for their brilliant collaboration and wonderful input into the book. A shoutout to David in particular for crafting a number of really unique insights for dads that we hope will really resonate and help with their own hypnobirthing journeys.

It's also been a real pleasure to collaborate with our hypnobirthing experts - Natalie Reed from Birthing Matters, and Jessica & Ben Lagrone from Balanced Families, who's unique perspective on hypnobirthing and the role of dads-to-be has been invaluable.

Finally a huge thanks to Lia Brigante from The Royal College of Midwives who has provided us with much inspiration and amazing learnings for the book.

RESOURCES

acog.org, The American College of Obstetricians and Gynecologists

americanpregnancy.org, American Pregnancy Association

babycenter.com, Baby Center

babycentre.co.uk, Baby Centre

cdc.gov, Centers for Disease Control

evidencebasedbirth.com, Evidence Based Birth

fda.gov, U.S. Food & Drug Administration

flo.health, Flo

healthline.com, Healthline

mayoclinic.org, Mayo Clinic

nhs.uk, National Health Service UK

parents.com, Parents

thebump.com, The Bump

us.hypnobirthing.com, Hypnobirthing International

verywellfamily.com, Verywell Family

whattoexpect.com, What to Expect

womenshealth.gov, U.S Department of Health & Human Services

REFERENCES

Miller, Siobhan. *Hypnobirthing: Practical Ways to Make Your Birth Better*. Hachette UK, 2019.

Mongan, Marie F. *Hypnobirthing: The Mongan Method: The Natural Approach to a Safe, Easier, More Comfortable Birthing*. Souvenir Press, 2020.

Murkoff, Heidi, and Charles J. Lockwood, MD. *What to Expect When You're Expecting*. New York: Workman Publishing, 2016.

Simkin, Penny, and Katie Rohs. *The Birth Partner: A Complete Guide to Childbirth for Dads, Doulas, and Other Labor Companions*. Harvard Common Press, 2018.

Printed in Great Britain
by Amazon

27412505R00128